Psychology

T0087469

Polity's *Why It Matters* series

In these short and lively books, world-leading thinkers make the case for the importance of their subjects and aim to inspire a new generation of students.

Helen Beebee & Michael Rush, *Philosophy*
Nick Couldry, *Media*
Robert Eaglestone, *Literature*
Andrew Gamble, *Politics*
Lynn Hunt, *History*
Tim Ingold, *Anthropology*
Katrin Kohl, *Modern Languages*
Neville Morley, *Classics*
Alexander B. Murphy, *Geography*
Geoffrey K. Pullum, *Linguistics*
Michael Schudson, *Journalism*
Ann B. Stahl, *Archaeology*
Graham Ward, *Theology and Religion*
Richard Wiseman, *Psychology*

Richard Wiseman

Psychology

Why It Matters

polity

First published in 2022 by Polity Press

Polity Press
65 Bridge Street
Cambridge CB2 1UR, UK

Polity Press
111 River Street
Hoboken, NJ 07030, USA

ISBN-13: 978-1-5095-5042-5
ISBN-13: 978-1-5095-5043-2 (pb)

A catalogue record for this book is available from the British Library.

Library of Congress Control Number: 2022933000

Typeset in 11 on 15pt Sabon
by Cheshire Typesetting Ltd, Cuddington, Cheshire
Printed and bound in the UK by CPI Group (UK) Ltd, Croydon

For further information on Polity, visit our website:
politybooks.com

Contents

Acknowledgements   vi

Introduction   1
1 How Does Your Mind Really Work?   6
2 A Unique Toolkit   23
3 Myth Busting   43
4 Informing and Resolving Debate   61
5 Creating a Better World   87
Conclusion   113

Notes   121
Further Reading   135

Acknowledgements

I would like to thank the many people who have provided information and helpful insights during the writing of this book: Geoffrey Dean, Greta Defeyter, Cara Flanagan, Mike Gazzaniga, Jules P. Harrell, Leonard Jason, Rob Jenkins, Helen Keen, Emma Ladds, Peter Lamont, Elizabeth Loftus, Peter Lovatt, Lois MacCullagh, Gabriele Oettingen, Adrian Owen, Richard Philpot, Stephen Reicher, Chris Skurka, Effua E. Sosoo, Kimberley Wade, Caroline Watt, David Yeager, and Sally Zlotowitz. In addition, special thanks to my wonderful editor, Pascal Porcheron, and the team at Polity.

Introduction

During my childhood, I used to regularly visit my grandfather. Although most of the trips were pleasant but uneventful, one of our meetings had a profound influence on my life. I was around eight years old, and my grandfather and I were enjoying a cup of tea in his living room. He handed me a black marker pen and a Victorian penny, and asked me to write my initials on the coin. My grandfather then placed the penny in the palm of his hand and closed his fingers around the coin. A few moments later, he whispered a magic word and then slowly opened his hand to reveal that the coin had disappeared. Next, he reached under his chair and took out a metal box that was about the size of a deck of cards. The lid of the box was held securely in place with several rubber bands. My grandfather handed over the box and asked me to open it. I removed the bands and opened the box, only to discover a slightly smaller metal box that was also sealed with several more rubber bands. Once again, I removed the bands and carefully opened the second box. This time I found a little green cloth bag. I looked inside the bag and, to my amazement, discovered my initialled penny.

I became hooked on conjuring and spent a lot of my youth reading as much about the topic as possible. By my early teens, I was performing magic on a regular basis and wanted to become a professional prestidigitator. However, as time went on, my plans began to change. A good magician needs to understand how audiences perceive the world. This involves knowing the type of events that capture people's attention, when and why they become suspicious, and how to ensure that certain parts of a performance vanish from their memories. The more I examined these topics, the more I became fascinated with the human mind.

I eventually went to University College London to study for an undergraduate degree in psychology. Towards the end of my time there, I happened to walk past a poster that caught my attention. Professor Robert Morris from the University of Edinburgh was carrying out work into psychics and mediums, and he wanted a Ph.D. student to investigate the psychology of deception. I successfully applied for the position, travelled up to Scotland and spent the next four years investigating magic, belief and the paranormal. After being awarded my doctorate, I was offered a lectureship in the Psychology Department at the University of Hertfordshire. I have been at the university ever since and am now a Professor of Psychology. During this time, I have researched a variety of areas, including the psychology of illusion, luck, conjuring, the paranormal, and lying. And all because my grandfather once showed me an amazing magic trick.

That's enough about me, let's talk about you. You are remarkable. Like most people, you can experience a vast range of thoughts and emotions, including falling in love, planning a holiday, feeling happy, becoming jealous, remembering last Tuesday, listening to music, contemplating the meaning of life, adding up a column of numbers, deciding what to order in a restaurant, dreaming, and reading overly long sentences like this one. You are also capable of carrying out an amazingly wide variety of behaviours, including walking along the street, juggling, singing a song, preparing breakfast, painting a picture, dancing until the small hours, riding a bicycle, yawning, sneezing, kissing, helping others, falling asleep, and laughing. Not only that, but you are the only person just like you in the entire world.

Psychologists have spent many years investigating this cornucopia of thoughts, feelings, and behaviours. Their work has been described in many different types of books. Textbooks have presented broad-brush overviews of vast swathes of research, academic monographs have outlined specific areas in considerable detail, popular books have provided accessible accounts of especially interesting ideas and findings, and self-help texts have offered pragmatic tips and techniques that aim to improve lives. This book adopts a somewhat different perspective and asks one of the most important questions of all: why does psychology matter?

In my experience, this is not an issue that is widely discussed in psychology. Students often learn about psychological methods and knowledge without reflecting on whether this work is meaningful. Similarly, academic psychologists are busy people, and sometimes rush from one project to another without thinking about whether, and how, their work matters. This book is an opportunity to take a breath, slow down and reflect on why psychologists do what they do.

Like any author, I am biased. I have devoted my entire career to researching, teaching, and promoting psychology, and this book is based on my experiences and presents my point of view. I should also say that I don't think that all psychology matters. In fact, some of the work is irrelevant, unimportant, and even harmful. However, when psychology is at its best, I believe that it is hugely meaningful. Each of the following chapters explores a different reason why I think that psychology matters and describes research projects that illustrate the diversity of work in that area. There is a vast body of potential research to choose from, and I have selected examples that I find especially compelling, interesting, uplifting, or impactful. In the conclusion, I will offer some practical suggestions for promoting even more meaningful work in the future.

I hope that you enjoy our time together.

I

How Does Your Mind Really Work?

Computers, washing machines and vaccum cleaners all arrive with manuals. Unfortunately, we aren't born with a guide to our mind and so we have to figure out what makes us tick. Over the years, psychologists have challenged many of our most cherished intuitions and common-sense ideas about how our minds work, and often discovered that we are more remarkable than we ordinarily imagine. In this chapter, we will explore several examples of this surprising, interesting, and counter-intuitive work. Along the way, we will encounter people dressed as gorillas and ghosts, discover what happened when people tried to remember 10,000 photographs, find out why psychologists have staged hundreds of mock accidents, and much more.

How Does Your Mind Really Work?

Looking at Observation

Most people believe that they are good observers and that they would instantly spot a striking event happening right in front of them. However, psychologists have discovered that there's far more to vision than meets the eye.

British researcher Tony Cornell, who was interested in the possible existence of ghosts, decided to find out what would happen if people came face to face with a seemingly supernatural spectre. In one study, Cornell dressed up in a white sheet and strolled down a path near a busy city centre. Amazingly, almost no one seemed to spot his ghostly figure. In another piece of research, Cornell visited his local cinema, put on his ghost costume, waited until a film was showing and then walked out in front of the screen. He then asked the audience if they had noticed anything strange and discovered that around a third of them had completely missed his apparitional appearance.[1]

In the 1970s, Ulric Neisser and colleagues conducted more systematic research into people's inability to see what's happening in front of them. Neisser created a short film containing two teams of people.[2] Each team consisted of three individuals, with those in one team wearing white tee-shirts and those in the other team wearing black tee-shirts. Each of the teams had their own basketball and during the film the players in each team constantly passed their basketball between one another. A few minutes into the film, a woman wearing a long black raincoat and carrying an open umbrella walked across the scene and through the players. Neisser showed the film to people and asked them to count the number of times that the players dressed in the white tee-shirts passed their basketball between one another. Amazingly, most people failed to spot the woman with the umbrella.

In the 1990s, Dan Simons and Christopher Chabris made several versions of Neisser's classic film and replaced the umbrella-holding woman with other unexpected events.[3] A member of their research team had recently conducted another experiment in which they had dressed up in a gorilla costume, and so in one of the films they put on the costume and walked through the basketball players. As a bonus, they even paused in the middle of the scene and beat their chest at the camera. Simons showed the film to people and asked them to count how many times the team wearing white tee-shirts passed their basketball. In line with Neisser's previous findings, around half of them failed to spot the gorilla.

Simons uploaded his wonderful gorilla film onto the internet, and it quickly became a viral hit. Inspired by both this work and my background in magic, I created a short online video called 'The Colour Changing Card Trick'. This film involved two people performing a card trick on a table. During the trick, the performers changed the colour of the tablecloth, their clothing, and the curtain behind them. Amazingly, most people watching the film fail to spot these changes. In another dramatic illustration of our ability to miss what is happening in front of our eyes, researchers discovered that students talking on a mobile telephone even failed to notice a clown riding past on a unicycle![4]

These studies have helped psychologists to understand more about the innermost workings of our visual system. According to one model of perception, processing all the incoming information from our surroundings would quickly overwhelm our visual system. Instead, our mind automatically and unconsciously focuses attention on what appears to be important. This process usually works well and allows us to gain an accurate impression of what is happening around us. However, under certain circumstances, this process can cause us to miss the unexpected. When we are watching a film in a cinema, we don't expect to see a ghost walk in

9

front of the screen. When we are asked to count the number of times people pass a basketball on a video, we are not looking out for someone dressed as a gorilla. And when we watch a card trick, we do not pay attention to the colour of the tablecloth, the performers' clothing, or the curtains. At one level, missing these striking events illustrates that our common-sense understanding of observation is deeply wrong. However, at another level, it demonstrates just how amazing and sophisticated our minds really are.

TOTAL RECALL

In the 1970s, Lionel Standing conducted a remarkable study into the power of memory. Standing persuaded five volunteers to spend several days looking at 10,000 photographs. The volunteers only saw each image for five seconds. To discover how many images they had remembered, the volunteers were shown several hundred photographs, and asked to identify the ones that they have seen in the earlier part of the study. Using this information, Standing estimated that the volunteers had remembered around 6,600 photographs, despite having only seen each of them for a few seconds. Similar work by Rob Jenkins and colleagues suggests that people have, on average, 5,000 faces stored in their memories. People often believe that they have a poor memory. In fact, most of us can store vast amounts of visual material, and researchers have used this remarkable ability to help people to pass exams, to remember online passwords, to deliver long speeches without notes, and much more.

Sources: L. Standing, 'Learning 10,000 pictures', *Quarterly Journal of Experimental Psychology*, 25, 207–222 (1973); R. Jenkins, A.J. Dowsett, & A.M. Burton, 'How many faces do people know?' *Proceedings. Biological Sciences*, 285(1888) (2018), 2018.1319.

Beliefs, Opinions, and Decisions

In the 1970s, Amos Tversky and Daniel Kahneman conducted a now classic experiment using just eight numbers.[5] They visited a high school and asked students to estimate the answer to one of two equations. Half of the students were asked to solve this equation:

$$8 \times 7 \times 6 \times 5 \times 4 \times 3 \times 2 \times 1 = ?$$

whilst the others were shown this equation:

$$1 \times 2 \times 3 \times 4 \times 5 \times 6 \times 7 \times 8 = ?$$

How Does Your Mind Really Work?

Mathematically, the two equations are identical and so, if the students were being logical, the two groups should have come up with the same answers. However, the students who saw the first equation produced estimates that were around four times larger than those who were presented with the second equation. Tversky and Kahneman speculated that the students had taken a mental shortcut and based their answers on the initial part of each equation. The first equation starts off with relatively large numbers and so the students came up with a high estimate. In contrast, the second equation starts with much smaller numbers and so the students produced a much lower estimate. Further work has shown that this effect, which is often referred to as 'anchoring', can influence our decisions in many situations. For example, a furniture shop might display a sign saying that a £500 chair has been reduced to £250. By anchoring on the first price, the second figure seems surprisingly low. Conversely, during a negotiation, one party might open with a low opening offer in order that their subsequent offers appear more impressive.

Other work has revealed that many of our beliefs, judgements, and decisions are clouded by similar sorts of biases. Take, for instance, the way in which we account for the events in our lives. Research shows that we tend to attribute the outcome of such events either to ourselves (e.g. our personality, intelligence, or abilities) or to external factors (e.g. other people, chance, or fate). So far, so good. However, the way in which we make these attributions depends upon the outcome of the event. When we succeed, we tend to take the credit ourselves ('I did well at the exam because I revised hard and I am intelligent'), whereas when we fail, we tend towards blaming external factors ('I failed because there were distractions in the exam hall').[6] On the upside, this bias can help us to feel good about ourselves, but on the downside, it can prevent us from taking responsibility for past errors and learning from them.

Once we have made a decision, or formed a belief, other types of biased thinking ensure that we are unlikely to change our mind. One of the most important of these can be illustrated with a simple game that you can play with your friends.[7] Tell your friend that you have a rule for generating sets of three numbers and the following sequence fits your rule: 2, 4, 8. Now ask them to discover your rule by generating new sequences and explain that you will tell them whether their responses fit the rule. Most people think that the rule involves doubling the number each time and so generate sequences that confirm this notion (such as 16, 32, 64 or 10, 20, 40). Over time, your friend will generate more and more confirming sequences and become increasingly confident that they are correct. In fact, their rule is wrong. It's only when they generate examples that disconfirm the doubling rule (such as 1, 5, 31 or 67, 37, 21) that they discover that the correct rule is that the sequence must contain ascending numbers.

This tendency to seek out information that confirms, rather than disconfirms, our views and opinions affects many areas of our lives. Imagine that you happen to believe that introverts enjoy reading books and that extroverts like participating in activities that get their adrenaline pumping. Now imagine going to a party and chatting to someone whom you haven't met before. This person reveals that they are an introvert and so you ask them if they have read any good books lately. Then, later in the evening, another guest describes themselves as an extrovert and so you ask them if they have ever tried skydiving. Your leading questions are likely to elicit information that confirms your pre-existing beliefs. In doing so, you are less likely to discover, for instance, that the first person is a bungee jumping fanatic and that the second guest has just devoured Tolstoy's *War and Peace*.[8] The same search for confirming information can also result in people maintaining inaccurate beliefs about many topics, including sport, news, politics, and religion. Recent work into this curious phenomenon suggests that this bias is amplified by social media because most of us are connected to people who share our thoughts and opinions.[9]

Finally, we might like to think that we admit the error of our ways when we eventually encounter information that obviously disconfirms our beliefs. Unfortunately, research suggests that under these circumstances we can misremember our original beliefs and convince ourselves that we were correct all along. Early work into this curious effect was carried out in the 1970s by Baruch Fischhoff and Ruth Beyth.[10] During the initial part of their study, participants were asked to think about Richard Nixon's forthcoming visit to China and the Soviet Union, and to predict the probability of various events happening on the trip, such as Nixon meeting Chairman Mao. Then, after Nixon's trip was finished and had been widely reported in the media, participants were asked to recall their initial predictions. Often the participants' prior thoughts had been wrong. However, rather than realizing that this was the case, they misremembered their initial responses and convinced themselves that they had been right all along. This effect is known as the 'hindsight bias', and hundreds of studies have shown that it can fool people into believing that they can accurately predict the stock market, foresee the outcome of elections and sporting events, figure out how long their friend's relationships will last, and much more.

On a more positive note, some of the most recent work in the area has investigated how to help people overcome these biases and make more rational decisions. For instance, Anne-Laure Sellier and colleagues asked a group of business students to play a video game in which they were a detective trying to find a missing person.[11] The game was designed to illustrate some of the biases described above, including, for example, how the students' search strategy was biased by their tendency to look for confirmatory evidence. Next, the students took part in a simulation exercise based around the fateful decision to launch the space shuttle *Challenger*. Compared to another group of students who had not been informed about such biases, the group who had played the game about irrational thinking were far less likely to make dangerous decisions surrounding the launch of the shuttle.

Most people like to think that they make up their minds about important issues in a rational way. However, the surprising truth is that our thoughts and beliefs are frequently the result of several unconscious biases. We are often swayed by the first information that we see, adopt certain beliefs because they make us feel good, look for information that confirms our opinions, and misremember the past to convince ourselves that we were right all along. On the upside, these mental shortcuts allow us to make decisions quickly and to function without having to constantly think about the best course of action. However, in some situations, these unconscious biases can result in serious and harmful beliefs and opinions, including those associated with sexism and racism. However, the good news is that research suggests that it is possible to overcome these biases, and so significantly improve our decision making and judgements. This work is another compelling illustration of how our common-sense understanding of the mind is incorrect, and how psychology provides important insights into how we really think.

FACE TIME

It's almost impossible to understand what's going on inside a baby's mind because they are unable to describe their thoughts and feelings. However, some researchers have tackled this issue by carrying out cleverly designed behavioural studies. One of the best-known examples uses a five feet square wooden box (known as a 'looking chamber') to examine babies' facial perception. Early work in this area involved researchers creating a drawing of a simple face (think two dots for eyes and a semi-circle for a smiling mouth) and another drawing containing the same elements but arranged in a random way. The researchers then put these two drawings inside the box, ensuring that one drawing was placed on the left-hand side and the other was placed on the right-hand side. Next, they carefully placed a baby inside the box and measured the amount of time that the baby spent looking at each of the pictures. This technique allows researchers to discover whether the baby could distinguish between the two pictures and, if this was the case, which one they found more interesting. Over the years, this technique has revealed a series of fascinating insights, including that most babies exhibit a strong preference for face-like images, and that they spend more time looking at faces in which the eyes are open rather than closed, are attractive, and are making direct eye contact rather than looking to the side. This research is a great illustration of how psychology can shine a light on inaccessible parts of the mind.

To Help or Not to Help, That Is the Question

In the late 1960s, John Darley and Bibb Latané conducted a ground-breaking series of studies examining helping behaviour.[12] Volunteers were invited to their laboratory to take part in a psychology experiment but then found themselves confronted with an apparent emergency. In one study, for instance, the volunteers were shown into a room and asked to complete a questionnaire. As they worked away, smoke started to leak into the room, suggesting that there was a nearby fire. In another study, it appeared that a volunteer was having an epileptic seizure. These emergencies were manufactured by the researchers. In the first instance the smoke was generated by a machine and in the second study the apparent volunteer was part of the research team. The researchers ensured that the participants were either alone in the laboratory or with a small group of other people, and secretly observed how they responded to the apparent emergency. Common sense predicts that the larger the number of people at the scene of an emergency, the greater the likelihood of a person stepping forward and helping. However, the results revealed the exact opposite: the greater the number of people at the scene of the emergency, the less likely it was that the person helped. For instance, in the smoke study, around 50% of the students working alone reported the smoke within a few minutes, versus only about 12% of those who were in the room with other people. This was even the case when the smoke became so thick that it obscured people's vision. This curious phenomenon has been replicated many times over the years and is referred to as the 'bystander effect'. It is a compelling illustration of how our behaviour is modified by the situation in which we find ourselves.

Although the bystander effect has been well established in hundreds of laboratory-based experiments, some psychologists have noted that people are often surprisingly helpful in some more realistic settings. For instance, in 2019, researchers analysed CCTV footage of violent situations occurring in public in the UK, South Africa, and the Netherlands, and discovered that in 90% of cases at least one person tried to help.[13]

Over the years, psychologists have proposed various explanations to account for the bystander effect. For instance, some have argued that it is due to a so-called 'diffusion of responsibility', wherein everyone decides that it is someone else's responsibility to help and so no-one acts. Other researchers have investigated the possibility that people tend not to help when they are around others because they are afraid of making a mistake or looking foolish. Other work has examined the idea that people think that they should do something, but also believe that the rest of the group do not share their opinion, and so they conform to what appears to be the social norm.

Another strand of research has examined the factors that enhance and diminish the effect. For instance, people are much more likely to help when the person in need is like them, when they feel a sense of personal responsibility, when they are not in a hurry and when they are in a good mood. One of the most recent studies in the area has examined the bystander effect within the context of cyber-bullying, and involved an under-researched cohort, namely Chinese students. The work, carried out by Angel Nga Man Leung, yielded several interesting findings, including showing that participants who had been cyberbullied in the past were more likely to stand up for victims in the future.[14]

Research into the bystander effect demonstrates that our common-sense ideas about how people act in social situations can be erroneous, and is an example of how psychologists have developed surprising insights into our actual behaviour.

Why Psychology Matters:
How Your Mind Really Works

In this chapter, we have encountered research that illustrates how psychology has challenged people's common-sense ideas about how their minds work. For instance, people often believe that they are good observers, make sound judgements, and have a poor memory. However, as we have seen, research shows that they often fail to see what is happening in front of their eyes, frequently hold irrational beliefs, and can recall significant amounts of visual material. As well as being theoretically important, this work has practical applications. For example, insights into observation have helped to assess eye-witness testimony in the courtroom, and research into unconscious biases has helped to combat sexist and racist beliefs. Over the years, psychologists have revealed a series of surprising, fascinating, and counter-intuitive insights into the way in which we think, feel, and behave. In addition, much of this work has revealed that our minds are far more complex and amazing than we ordinarily imagine.

2

A Unique Toolkit

In the previous chapter, we examined some of the many fascinating, and counter-intuitive, insights that psychology provides into the human mind. We are now going to examine how researchers go about conducting the work that underpins these discoveries. Contrary to popular belief, psychologists don't tend to analyse people's dreams, show them strange inkblots, or ask them what comes to mind when they hear the word 'banana'. Instead, they have developed a far more reliable set of techniques for studying the human mind. This unique toolkit is remarkably flexible and allows researchers to investigate every aspect of the human psyche. In addition, understanding these techniques provides people with a set of thinking skills that are important and useful in everyday life. In this chapter, we will explore this toolkit by carrying out several imaginary studies that will involve you interviewing one of your closest friends, heading to your local high street, secretly observing people in a cinema, and transforming your house into a laboratory. Although psychologists tend to examine important issues, I thought that it would be fun to have our imaginary studies investigate a more light-hearted topic. So, prepare to encounter a series of terrible puns as we attempt to answer a question that has probably never taxed the minds of the world's greatest thinkers: does watching horror films cause people to eat more popcorn?

Starting Out

Imagine that you decide to spend an evening watching a film. Armed with a tub of popcorn, you curl up on your sofa and press play on *Dracula vs the Wolfman VI: Fangs for the Memories*. After the film has ended, you notice something rather odd. You normally eat around half a tub of popcorn during a film; however, this time you have consumed the entire tub. Intrigued, you wonder whether the scary nature of the film may have caused you to eat more popcorn than usual. In doing so, you have just carried out a key part of any psychological inquiry, namely identifying a research topic.

A Unique Toolkit

Being of a curious disposition, you decide to put your popcorn-based hypothesis to the test. Fortunately, your good friend Sally runs a Dracula fan club. You contact Sally and the two of you spend hours chatting about the amount of popcorn that she has consumed whilst watching different types of films. After thinking back over the past few years, she eventually concludes that she has indeed eaten more popcorn during scary films.

This type of work is often referred to as a case study, and these usually involve an in-depth investigation with a single person or small group of people. Over the years, psychologists have used this approach to examine a diverse range of topics. For instance, around 1800, French physicians discovered a young boy who appeared to have spent several years living alone in a forest. Despite repeated attempts to teach the boy how to converse, he was unable to speak fluently. Researchers at the time argued that the case suggested that early interaction with other humans was vital for language acquisition (some modern-day psychologists have contested this conclusion). Another famous case study comes from the 1950s and involved a man named Henry Molaison. When he was in his twenties, Molaison underwent brain surgery to treat epilepsy, but after the operation he was unable to remember any new information or experiences. Constantly living in the present, he participated in psychological studies for almost fifty years, and helped researchers to identify the parts of the brain that appear to be associated with the creation and retrieval of new memories.

QUALITATIVE RESEARCH

A great deal of psychology involves asking people to complete questionnaires, make decisions, carry out tasks, and so on. Because this work focuses on numbers and measurement, it's usually referred to as the 'quantitative' approach. In contrast, 'qualitative' research adopts a somewhat different perspective, and often aims to obtain a rich and detailed representation of people's opinions, thoughts, beliefs, and experiences. Other qualitative work looks at people's conversations and comments, and examines, for instance, how they talk to one another, describe themselves and make requests. Qualitative work usually takes place outside of the laboratory, frequently entails analysing interviews or texts for key themes, patterns, and ideas, and often involves reporting results in participants' own voices. Case studies frequently adopt a qualitative approach.

The qualitative approach can be used to study a wide range of topics. Researchers might, for instance, interview people from different cultural backgrounds about their experience of stress, talk to teenagers about how social media shapes their sense of identity, explore neurodiversity in the workplace, examine the language used by medics in hospitals, or work with teachers to understand the challenges of delivering a new school curriculum. Qualitative work has yielded important insights into people's perspectives, experiences and behaviour, and is a useful tool for reflecting the complexity surrounding an issue.

A large amount of work in academic psychology, and nearly all of my own research, adopts a quantitative approach, and so much of this book reflects that perspective.

Case studies are an effective way of gaining a detailed insight into an individual or a small group. However, like all methods within psychology, the approach isn't perfect. For instance, because case studies are usually based on a small number of people, it's possible that the findings do not generalize to others. In our imaginary study, your lengthy conversation with Sally was a good way of finding out about her popcorn consumption during various films. However, you contacted Sally because she loves horror films and so it's possible that her experiences may not apply to other people. With this issue in mind, you decide to carry out some more research.

Heading to the High Street

The following day, you put on your jacket, pick up a clipboard and head to the high street. Standing on a busy corner, you ask hundreds of passers-by to think about the last time that they saw a film, and to rate both how much popcorn they consumed and the scariness of the film. Not everyone has the time to chat, but lots of people are kind enough to answer your questions. You then analyse your data and discover that your hypothesis has been confirmed: the scarier the film, the greater the amount of popcorn consumed. Over the years, these types of surveys have yielded fascinating insights into a variety of psychological phenomena, including work suggesting that poor sleep is associated with spending lots of time on your smartphone, that increased exercise is related to greater happiness, and that people who enjoy gardening are less stressed.[1]

However, your street survey also has its shortcomings. For instance, although the work involved far more people than your case study with Sally, the results may still not generalize to others. After all, you could only involve people who had the time to speak to you and so the findings may not apply to those with busier lives.

Then there is also the all-important issue of measurement. When people complete questionnaires or are interviewed, they are asked to report their thoughts, opinions, beliefs, emotions, and behaviour. Unfortunately, sometimes people can struggle to provide reliable information. For instance, would you be able to remember how happy you were last year? Or accurately rate how well you slept last week? Or be comfortable telling researchers about the last time that you broke the law? Similarly, during our imaginary street survey, the passers-by might have struggled to accurately rate how much popcorn they had consumed whilst watching various films. Eager to please, they might have come up with a rating, but that number may not be especially meaningful or accurate. In any study, it's important that researchers employ measures that are both meaningful and accurate. This isn't just an issue when it comes to asking people questions on the street. In fact, it applies to all psychological research.

Mindful of these issues, you decide to carry out a third piece of imaginary research.

A Unique Toolkit

Going Undercover

You head down to your local cinema and discover that they are showing another scary horror film: *Dracula vs the Wolfman VII: Coffin Up Blood*. You buy a ticket, sit towards the back of the auditorium, and secretly note down the amount of popcorn consumed by the people watching the film. Next, you repeat the process during a romantic comedy. Much like an encounter with Dracula, it's a pain in the neck. However, compared to the street survey, your measurement of popcorn consumption feels far more meaningful and accurate. Not only that, but you know that the people in one group were watching a scary film and those in the other group were watching a romantic comedy. Study completed, you race home, examine your data using various statistical tests, and discover that people ate more popcorn during the scary film than the romantic comedy.

This study involved observing people's everyday behaviour, and over the years, researchers have used this approach in a diverse range of contexts. For instance, Robert Levine and Ara Norenzayan thought that there might be a link between people rushing around and them having a heart attack.[2] To find out if this was the case, they arranged for researchers in over thirty countries to head out into the street and secretly record the time it took people to walk sixty feet, and then compared these measurements to the rate of death from coronary heart disease in each country. Faster average walking speeds were associated with higher death rates. In other studies, researchers have looked at records of people's everyday behaviour, such as CCTV footage or databases. For instance, Mark Frank and Thomas Gilovich thought that the colour of the outfits worn by sports teams might be related to their performance.[3] As black uniforms are commonly associated with authoritarianism, the researchers speculated that teams wearing such outfits would be more aggressive and so receive more warnings from referees. The researchers trawled through records from both the American National Football League and National Hockey League and discovered support for their hypothesis. These types of studies are great for finding out how people behave in the real world, and frequently involve measures that seem meaningful.

However, as you think about the information that you collected in the cinema, another issue comes to mind. Your data showed that the people watching the scary film consumed more popcorn, and so you concluded that the nature of the film affected their popcorn consumption. But there is another possibility, namely that people who go to scary films are especially fond of popcorn. In short, if Factor A is related to (or, to use the technical phrase, 'correlated with') Factor B, it doesn't mean that Factor A causes Factor B. In fact, Factor B may cause Factor A. This difference between correlation and causation is a potential issue with lots of the work that we have already discussed. Maybe people's sleep is disrupted by them staring at their smartphone all day, or perhaps people with poor sleep tend to spend lots of time on their smartphone. Maybe exercise makes people happy or perhaps being happy makes people exercise more. When it comes to speed of walking and death from coronary heart disease, maybe rushing around increases the likelihood of a heart attack, or maybe people who are prone to heart attacks rush around. Similarly, maybe wearing a black outfit causes a sports team to play more aggressively or perhaps more aggressive teams choose to wear black. To make matters slightly more complicated, it's also possible that any correlation between two factors might be due to a third factor. The internet is full of fun examples that illustrate this notion, including the fact that the amount of serious crime committed in major cities is related to the amount of ice cream sold by street vendors (both increase in the

CHOOSING A RESEARCH TOPIC

In our imaginary studies, the idea of scary films driving popcorn consumption arose because you noticed something unusual in your everyday life. This also happens in psychology. However, there are several other reasons why researchers might choose to investigate a topic. They might, for instance, want to test a theory, solve a practical problem, explore an important societal issue, try to help others, or evaluate an intriguing claim. The topics that psychologists examine, and the ways in which they undertake this work, are influenced by several factors, including past research, the prevailing zeitgeist, the availability of funding, and the researcher's beliefs and perspectives. When evaluating any study, it's often important to think about why researchers may have chosen to investigate a particular topic. Are they intrinsically interested in it? Or trying to make the world a better place? Or hoping to find support for a political or religious belief? Or wishing to advance a particular worldview or social policy? These sorts of questions can help to provide a more rounded view of the research.

summer months), and that children's shoe size is related to their reading level (both are related to the child's age).

Displaying the type of dogged determination that is key to success in psychology, you decide to carry out a fourth and final imaginary study.

Back Home

This last piece of imaginary research involves transforming your house into a laboratory. You paint the letter 'A' on your lounge door and the letter 'B' on your bedroom door. Next, you place a television and some weighing scales in each room and invite some friends over for the night. You give each person a big tub of popcorn as they arrive and toss a coin. If the coin comes up 'heads', then they are shown into Room A, and if it comes up 'tails', then they go to Room B. Everyone in Room A watches a very scary film (*Dracula vs the Wolfman VIII: Adventures in Cape Town*) whilst those in Room B see a romantic comedy. By weighing the amount of popcorn remaining in Room A and comparing it with the amount left in Room B, you can determine whether watching the scary film caused people to eat more popcorn. Once again, you analyse your data and find out that, as predicted, those in Room A ate more popcorn than those in Room B.

This study illustrates the basic elements associated with the experimental method. The experiment involved a relatively large group of people and so the results are likely to generalize to others. You weighed the amount of popcorn consumed and so the measurement is likely to be accurate and meaningful. And by randomly allocating people to watch one film or another, you ensured that any difference in popcorn consumption must be the result of them watching different films. As a result, you can separate correlation from causation. However, like the studies that you have carried out so far, the experiment isn't perfect. For instance, these types of experiments are often carried out in the somewhat artificial setting of the laboratory (or, in this instance, your house) and so the findings may not reflect what happens in the real world. In addition, the experiment only used two films, and you might want to repeat it with several other scary movies and romantic comedies to discover whether you always obtain the same results. Despite these shortcomings, the experimental approach is an extremely popular and powerful technique in psychology.

My guess is that if we were to run this final imaginary experiment for real, those who saw the scary film would indeed consume more popcorn. Why? Because in 2019, a similar experiment was carried out by Lama Mattar and colleagues.[4] In Mattar's study, participants were randomly assigned to watch either a scary film or a romantic comedy. Before seeing the film, they were handed a tray of snacks (including popcorn) and told that they could eat whatever they wanted. Those watching the scary film consumed significantly more fatty and salty items than those watching the romantic comedy.

Not So Fast

All four pieces of imaginary research used a different technique and yet yielded the same result. Psychologists refer to this as converging evidence (or triangulation), and these findings might tempt you to conclude that scary films do indeed make people eat more popcorn. Not so fast.

It's important to remember that you conducted all of the work. Throughout the studies, you probably wanted your hypothesis to be true, and so may have somehow influenced your participants to provide the responses that you wanted. The same applies in psychology (and much of science). It isn't enough that just one researcher has conducted some studies and reported positive results. Instead, it's important that lots of other researchers also carry out the same studies to see if they obtain similar results. It's especially good if the researchers carrying out this work don't share your love of the hypothesis, so that we can rule out the possibility of any effects being due to participants being unduly influenced. This idea (known as 'replication') has become an especially important issue over the past few years, with some researchers casting doubt on several well-known psychological findings because they have proved difficult to repeat. Let's return to our imaginary studies and assume that you ask several friends to re-stage your work into popcorn consumption and scary films. They patiently carry out similar research and obtain the same results. Can you finally conclude that your hypothesis is correct? Again, not so fast.

Your case study involved your friend Sally; the survey was carried out on a nearby high street; you observed people at your local cinema; the experimental study involved your friends; and the replications were conducted by people whom you know. In each instance, the data were collected from people who are, broadly speaking, like you. It might be reasonable to conclude that the hypothesis seems to be true among the type of people who were involved in the studies and the culture in which they were conducted, but it's important not to over-generalize your findings. After all, it's quite possible that you would obtain a different set of results if you were to involve people from more diverse backgrounds and cultures. Cultural factors affect the hypotheses that researchers examine, the participants whom they involve in their research and the measures that they use. This is an important issue in psychology because most studies (including many of those discussed in this book) involve participants drawn from Western, Educated, Industrialized, Rich, and Democratic societies (thus the acronym 'WEIRD'). Fortunately, this issue is now being addressed, with an increasing number of studies involving more diverse researchers, cohorts, and cultures.

There is one final issue. Even if our imaginary studies suggest that scary films cause people to eat more popcorn, they haven't explored why this is the case. Finding out what causes the effect requires generating and testing more hypotheses. For instance, you might speculate that scary films make people feel anxious, and that they eat more popcorn to calm down. To test this idea, you could measure people's anxiety by monitoring their physiology as they watched a horror film and see whether popcorn consumption happens at especially scary moments. Alternatively, you might think that seeing images of actors screaming in terror primes people to put more popcorn in their mouths. To test this hypothesis, you might identify moments in the film associated with screaming and see if they are associated with popcorn consumption. Or you might start to examine whether the effect is especially prevalent among certain types of people (such as those of a nervous disposition) and use this information to help to shape your theory. Slowly but surely, this type of work will help to reveal the explanation for the phenomenon.

Having carried out this work, you are finally able to write up your studies and submit a paper to an academic journal. Other psychologists will then be asked to assess the quality of your work and will only allow it to be published if they are satisfied that it has sufficient merit. This process (known as peer review) isn't perfect, but it does ensure some level of quality control.

Why Psychology Matters: A Unique Toolkit

We set out to discover whether watching a scary film promotes popcorn consumption. Our imaginary research quickly revealed that answering this seemingly straightforward question was more complex than it first appeared. We carried out four studies to examine the issue and these involved interviewing Sally, conducting a survey on a nearby high street, secretly observing people in your local cinema, and staging an experiment in your house. None of these studies provided a perfect way of testing hypotheses. Instead, each one had its advantages and disadvantages. Psychology is the art of choosing the best method, or methods, for examining the question at hand, and then being open about the strengths and weaknesses of this work. This process can be messy, takes time and often involves making judgements in the face of uncertainty. As such, it should be approached with a sense of humility, a tolerance for ambiguity and an open mind. Psychology doesn't always provide the right answers. However, it does give us the best guess at any given moment. Moreover, when it hits the bullseye, psychology yields stunning insights into the human mind, improves people's lives, and provides effective solutions to important issues.

Understanding the types of methodological issues discussed in this chapter also helps people to critically assess any psychological study. Why did researchers choose to study this topic and how did they address the issue? Was this a quantitative or qualitative study? What method, or methods, were employed? Was the study carried out in an artificial setting? How many participants were involved and how were they recruited? What was measured during the study, and are these measurements meaningful and accurate? Has there been a confusion between correlation and causation? What theories have researchers used to account for their data and are other explanations possible? Have the results been replicated by other researchers? Is it reasonable to generalize the findings to other people and situations, especially within the context of more diverse populations and cultures? Has the work been peer reviewed?

Academics use this unique skillset to cast a sceptical eye over their own studies and (more commonly) the work of their colleagues. This type of critical thinking is also vitally important in everyday life. Spend any time watching television, reading books and articles, listening to the radio, visiting websites or on social media and you will find yourself being bombarded with psychological data. Journalists describe the latest scientific findings from psychology. Governments issue reports about new social policies. Self-help gurus present studies to promote new diets or healthier lifestyles. Advertisers and marketeers offer research to demonstrate the efficacy of new products or services. Writers cite work that supports their political perspectives and religious beliefs. Being able to assess these claims in a considered and critical way is a vital life skill, and helps people to make more informed decisions, to identify fake news, to avoid being scammed by dodgy advertisements, and much more.

In short, psychologists have developed a unique toolkit for studying the mind. Understanding these techniques equips people with a set of critical thinking skills that are essential in both academia and everyday life. In the previous chapter, we discovered how research using these methods reveals important insights into the human mind. In the next chapter, we will find out how they also allow psychologists to engage in a spot of myth busting.

3

Myth Busting

Magazines, newspapers, social media, and websites frequently contain information about psychology. As a result, the public are constantly bombarded with fascinating facts about the human mind, quizzes and questionnaires that claim to reveal the real them, and copious amounts of advice on how to improve their lives. Psychologists have examined some of the most enduring and widely believed claims, and frequently discovered that they are little more than myths. In this chapter, we will look at several examples of this important work, including the truth about lie detection, whether you only use 10% of your brain, and whether your future is written in the stars.

Myth Busting

Would I Lie to You?

Throughout history, people have tried to devise ways of discovering whether someone is being economical with the truth. Some of this work has examined whether it's possible to detect lying by monitoring people's physiology. Experimental research into this idea began in the 1920s, and involved psychologists helping to create polygraph machines that recorded people's blood pressure whilst they were being interrogated. Over the years, researchers working in this area have developed more sophisticated apparatus and devised several forms of questioning. However, many psychologists have queried the accuracy of this approach, noting, for instance, that some deceivers don't become anxious when they are lying and that some truth tellers become nervous when connected to such devices.[1] Despite such scepticism, polygraph machines still frequently appear in films and on television shows, and so the public continue to believe that they are a fool-proof way of discovering whether someone is lying.

Some researchers and writers have taken a different approach, and claimed that lying is reliably associated with certain types of body language and facial expressions. One of the most widely believed ideas focuses on people's eye movements, and suggests that they are more likely to look up to their right when they are lying, and more likely to look up to their left when they are telling the truth. A few years ago, my colleagues and I put this claim to the test.[2]

In our first study, students were handed a mobile telephone and asked to take it into a nearby office. Half of the students were instructed to place the telephone in an office cupboard whilst the other half were asked to hide it in their pocket. The students were then asked to try to convince an interviewer that they had placed the telephone in the cupboard. This procedure ensured that half of the students were telling the truth during the interviews and that half of them were lying. We filmed the interviews, and then carefully counted the number of times that each student looked up to their right and left. We found no evidence that lying or truth telling was reliably associated with either pattern of eye movement.

In a second study, we moved outside of the laboratory. During high-profile missing person cases, the police sometimes encourage family members to hold a press conference and to appeal for information about their missing relative. In a few of these cases, compelling evidence later emerges to suggest that one of the family members at the press conference was guilty of the crime and was therefore lying during the appeal. We obtained films of press conferences in which the relative had been subsequently shown to be either lying or telling the truth, and then counted the number of times their eyes moved up to the left or right. Once again, the findings didn't support the idea that the liars or truth tellers were especially likely to look in a particular direction.

Research examining how lying affects other types of verbal and non-verbal behaviour has yielded more positive results, with some work suggesting that liars tend to say less, reduce their use of first-person pronouns, hesitate more, and sound tense.[3] Although most of this work has been carried out within the West, some research has involved more diverse cohorts and cultures. For instance, two large-scale international studies (with participants drawn from over seventy countries and speaking more than forty languages) examined commonly held perceptions about behavioural changes associated with lying.[4] The work revealed some cultural differences but also a general belief that liars tend to avert their gaze.

In short, the notion that liars look up to their right is not supported by science. Nevertheless, the public continue to believe this myth and remain largely unaware of research that has identified more reliable behavioural indicators of deception.

DO YOU REALLY ONLY USE 10% OF YOUR BRAIN?

William James helped to lay the foundations for academic psychology in America. Born in 1842 in New York City, James spent much of his career at Harvard University studying a variety of fascinating topics, including the paranormal, consciousness and the will to believe. Many researchers believe that James may have also unwittingly made another equally lasting, but less valuable, contribution to psychology. In 1906, he delivered a speech to the American Philosophical Association and noted: 'We are making use of only a small part of our possible mental and physical resources.' The sentence is not especially contentious and almost certainly correct. However, James' remark appears to have become exaggerated over the years and slowly morphed into the notion that we only use 10% of our brains.

A few years ago, Barry Beyerstein outlined several strands of research questioning this popular myth. For instance, Beyerstein noted that if the 10% idea were true, then damaging the brain would be unlikely to have any significant consequences. In fact, people often experience profound changes to their thinking and behaviour after experiencing trauma to relatively small areas of their brain. Second, researchers have monitored brain activity during a variety of tasks (such as remembering a list of words or having a dream) and discovered that virtually every part of the brain shows some degree of activity during most of these tasks. Third, a significant amount of research has involved placing electrodes into the brain and measuring the activity of individual cells. These studies have shown widespread activation across the brain. In short, the notion that we only use 10% of our brains might be widely believed by the public, but it's little more than a myth.

Source: B.L. Beyerstein, 'Whence cometh the myth that we only use 10% of our brains?' in S. Della Sala (Ed.), *Mind Myths: Exploring Popular Assumptions About the Mind and Brain* (pp. 3–24), London: Wiley, 1999.

Written in the Stars

Astrologers create 'birth charts' (maps of the heavens as seen from where and when a person was born) and claim that they can use these to gain insights into the owner's character and major life events. This notion has been tested under controlled conditions by psychologists since the 1950s and the outcome of these studies is quite consistent.

Some of this work has involved having astrologers create a person's horoscope, presenting them with biographical profiles of several individuals (including the person whose horoscope they have just created), and asking them which profile best matches the horoscope. If the astrologer's claims are correct, they should consistently select the profile of the person whose horoscope they drew up. However, the results from several studies are consistent with chance guessing. In other studies, astrologers are provided with several people's birth dates and asked to create a horoscope for each one. These horoscopes are then shown to the individuals concerned and they are asked to select the horoscope that most accurately describes them. If astrology is valid, the individuals should be able to reliably identify their own horoscope. Once again, the findings from several studies are at chance.

On a more general level, media astrologers often publish columns that give brief daily, weekly, monthly, or yearly forecasts for each star sign. Research shows that people are unable to reliably identify their own forecast when the sun sign labels are removed. For instance, in one study, nearly 700 students were presented with unlabelled forecasts for the previous day and asked to pick the one that most accurately corresponded to events in their life.[5] The students' success rate was slightly worse than chance.

Some of the more subtle tests of astrology have involved 'time twins'. According to astrology, people born close together in time and geography should be closely similar to one another. To test this notion, Geoffrey Dean and Ivan Kelly examined the details of 2,100 people who had been born in London in early 1958.[6] Over 70% were born five minutes apart or less, and only 4% were born more than fifteen minutes apart. The database had over 100 relevant measures for each individual when they were aged eleven, sixteen and twenty-three, including their test scores, parent or teacher ratings, self-ratings of ability, and physical data. Dean and Kelly arranged the individuals in order of birth and moved through the list calculating the degree of similarity between each pair of people for each measure. They found that the predicted similarities did not exist. In fact, people who were born at the same moment were no more alike than those born much further apart in time.

But if astrology isn't true, why do so many people believe that their birth chart readings are accurate? Part of the answer lies in a study conducted by

Bertram Forer in the 1940s.[7] In this now classic study, Forer first obtained a newsstand astrology book and selected a few sentences like the following:

> You have a need for other people to like and admire you, and yet you tend to be critical of yourself. You have considerable unused capacity that you have not turned to your advantage. At times you have serious doubts as to whether you have made the right decision or done the right thing. You also pride yourself as an independent thinker, and do not accept others' statements without satisfactory proof. At times you are extroverted, affable and sociable, while at other times you are introverted, wary and reserved. Some of your aspirations tend to be rather unrealistic.

Forer had university students complete a personality test. He then told them that they were being given a unique personality description based on their scores, but in reality he gave each student the paragraph that he had prepared before the study. Remarkably, almost every student felt it was highly accurate. This finding has been replicated many times over the years, with additional studies examining why people find such statements to be so applicable. There are several factors at play. For instance, some statements are flattering ('You have considerable unused capacity'), whilst others contain opposites ('affable and sociable' yet 'wary and reserved'). Like astrological readings, readers see them as personally valid without realizing that they apply to most people. Other work has shown that people also tend to be impressed by the seemingly accurate parts of the reading and overlook the inaccurate sections and be blinded by meaningless jargon.

Personally, I am not convinced that astrology genuinely works, but I am a Virgo, and we are known for being sceptical.

EAT POPCORN

Many websites describe a remarkable experiment about subliminal advertising. According to these accounts, American market researcher James Vicary visited a cinema in the 1950s and arranged to have the phrases 'Drink Coke' and 'Eat Popcorn' briefly flashed up on the screen during a film. The images were only projected for a fraction of a second and so were not consciously seen by the audience. Nevertheless, these secret messages apparently resulted in a substantial increase in both beverage and food sales.

Intrigued by these findings, several researchers conducted their own studies into the alleged power of subliminal advertising but failed to find any significant effects. Why did Vicary's study apparently obtain positive results whilst subsequent experiments failed to demonstrate the power of subliminal advertising? Many years later, Vicary admitted that his study only involved a handful of people and was not very well conducted. In fact, some researchers have suggested that it was a hoax and may not have taken place at all.

Sources: T.E. Moore, 'Subliminal perception: Facts and fallacies', *Skeptical Inquirer*, 16 (1992), 273–281; M.L. De Fleur & R.M. Petranoff, 'A televised test of subliminal persuasion', *Public Opinion Quarterly*, 23 (1959), 168–180.

The Myth of Memory

Many people believe that their memories are an accurate account of past events. However, a large amount of psychological research has revealed that this is a myth. One early experiment into the topic was conducted in the 1950s, and involved students who had watched an American university football game between two college teams, Dartmouth and Princeton. The match proved especially rough, resulting in players suffering from various fractures and broken bones. After the game, Albert Hastorf and Hadley Cantril interviewed the two sets of fans and discovered that they had very different memories of the match.[8] For instance, around 30% of the Dartmouth fans thought that their team had initiated the rough tactics, whereas over 80% of the Princeton fans believed that this was the case. Similarly, less than 10% of the Dartmouth fans thought that their team were overly rough, compared to over 30% of the Princeton fans. These types of findings have been obtained in many memory experiments, and show how people's beliefs and preconceptions can cause them to misremember the past. There is also a tendency for such inaccuracies to grow over time, with some research suggesting that when people remember an event, they are often basing their recall on the last description of the event, rather than on their original experience.

Other work has shown that it's possible for people to develop extremely detailed, but entirely false, memories. In one study, for instance, Kimberley Wade and colleagues asked people to participate in a study about their childhood memories.[9] The researchers secretly used a photograph of each participant as a young child to create a fake image of them going on a ride in a hot-air balloon. Over the course of several interviews, the participants were shown the fake photograph and asked to describe their memory of this non-existent event. In the initial interviews, most participants said that they couldn't remember the trip. The researchers urged them to try harder, and by the final interview around half of the participants produced detailed descriptions of the fictitious balloon ride. Wade's work built on the pioneering research of Elizabeth Loftus and others, who persuaded participants to recall other childhood events that didn't take place, including becoming lost in a shopping mall, being hospitalized with a high fever, and accidentally ruining a wedding reception by knocking over a large bowl of punch.[10]

Although some of our memories are accurate, many of them are distorted and unreliable. Indeed, memory researcher Ulric Neisser likened the act of recall to a palaeontologist digging up a few dinosaur bones and then using these to try to figure out what the dinosaur looked like. The process involves a great deal of speculation and guesswork. As a result, it is open to bias and can even result in detailed descriptions of events that never happened.

THE NEED FOR MYTH BUSTING

Kelly Macdonald and colleagues have discovered that a surprisingly large number of people believe in mind myths. In one study, they asked over 3,000 members of the public to rate the degree to which they believed statements that described various psychological phenomena. Some of the phenomena were supported by science whilst others were complete myths. The participants were convinced that many of the myths were true. For instance, over 75% of the public thought that seeing letters backwards is a common sign of dyslexia (it isn't) and over 35% were convinced that people only use 10% of their brains (they don't).

Worryingly, the work also showed high levels of belief among teachers and neuroscience graduates, with, for instance, over 30% of the teachers believing that people only use 10% of their brains and 50% of the neuroscientists endorsing the dyslexia item. In similar work, Richard Bailey and colleagues had over 500 sports coaches complete a survey in which they indicated their level of knowledge about neuroscience and rated the validity of six myths (e.g. that we only use 10% of our brains). Overall, the coaches endorsed just over 40% of the myths. Even more worryingly, the coaches who claimed to have a higher level of knowledge about the brain endorsed more of the myths! Surprised by these high levels of belief, some psychologists have started to explore why such myths survive and prosper, with some work suggesting that people tell others about them to sound especially knowledgeable.

Sources: K. Macdonald, L. Germine, A. Anderson, J. Christodoulou, & L.M. McGrath, 'Dispelling the myth: Training in education or neuroscience decreases but does not eliminate beliefs in neuromyths', *Frontiers in Psychology*, 8 (2017), 1314; R.P. Bailey, D.J. Madigan, E. Cope, & A.R. Nicholls, 'The prevalence of pseudo-scientific ideas and neuromyths among sports coaches', *Frontiers in Psychology*, 9 (2018), 641; H. Mercier, Y. Majima, & H. Miton, 'Willingness to transmit and the spread of pseudoscientific beliefs', *Applied Cognitive Psychology*, 32 (2018), 499–505.

Perfect You

Many self-help gurus claim that visualizing your perfect life will significantly increase the likelihood of your dreams becoming a reality. Several studies have examined the impact of this type of exercise and the results are surprising. For instance, Lien Pham and Shelley Taylor worked with students to examine the effect of visualization on exam success.[11] Some students were asked to spend a few moments each day imagining obtaining a good grade in a forthcoming exam, whilst others weren't asked to carry out any form of visualization exercise. Those carrying out the visualization exercise ended up spending less time studying and obtained lower marks.

Other studies into the topic have been carried out by Gabriele Oettingen. In one study, Oettingen and her colleague Doris Mayer asked final-year students to record how frequently they visualized being offered their dream job after graduation and then tracked the group for two years. The more the students fantasized about success, the *less* likely they were to submit job applications and the less they earned two years later. Another study examined the effects of visualization on students' love lives.[12] Oettingen and Mayer assembled a group of students who had a secret crush on a classmate and asked them to describe what they thought would happen in a series of imaginary scenarios, such as bumping into the love of their lives on the street. Students rated their own responses for how positively they experienced their imagery. For instance, a student would give themselves a positive score if they imagined an ideal date, but a lower score if they imagined feeling anxious as they approached the person they admired. The researchers tracked the group for a few months, and discovered that those engaging in more positive fantasies were *less* likely to have made any progress towards developing a relationship with their dream partner.

Some researchers have suggested that visualizing your perfect life means that you are not mentally preparing yourself for the struggles and obstacles that may lay ahead. Others think that the visualization exercise may demotivate people by suggesting that they have already obtained their goal. Either way, these findings suggest imagining your dream life may make you feel better, but is unlikely to make those dreams come true.

But this is not to say that visualization isn't a powerful tool. In a separate part of Pham and Taylor's study into exam success, another group of students were asked to imagine themselves doing the types of activity associated with exam success, such as going to the library and studying. These students reported spending lots of time revising and eventually obtained higher exam grades than either the students in the control group or those who were simply imagining doing well in the exam. This technique (known as 'process visualization') involves imagining carrying out steps needed to achieve a goal, and research shows that it's far more effective than simply dreaming about your perfect life.[13]

Why Psychology Matters: Myth Busting

There is no reliable scientific evidence to support many widely believed claims about the human mind and behaviour, including the notion that looking left or right is a reliable guide to lying, that we only use 10% of our brains, or that memories are always an accurate account of past events. Surveys show that a large percentage of the public also believe many other highly questionable ideas, including the notion that people are either right-brained or left-brained, that hypnosis is an effective way of revealing past lives, that subliminal advertising is effective, and that people diagnosed with schizophrenia have multiple personalities. Research in this area is especially important because these myths can negatively impact on people's lives. For instance, it's easy to imagine how they could cause someone to wrongly accuse their friends of lying, or to waste valuable time using ineffective visualization techniques, or to visit a hypnotist to unlock their hidden memories. When it comes to mind myths, sorting science fact from science fiction is vital and is another reason why psychology matters.

4

Informing and Resolving Debate

Philosophers, politicians, theologians, writers, historians, scientists, and many others have long debated a wide range of psychological issues. These arguments have focused on several important topics, including whether humans really have free will; how brains generate consciousness; why people commit crime; the nature of ethnicity and gender; whether psychic ability exists; the best way of educating children; whether playing violent video games makes people more aggressive; what happens during sleep and dreaming; whether some groups of people are more intelligent than others; the nature of good and evil; and the extent to which humans are a product of their genes and upbringing. Psychologists have conducted research that has helped to inform and resolve these debates. In this chapter, we will explore several examples of this fascinating work, including research into the existence of psychic ability, how best to conceptualize the human mind, and the nature of consciousness.

Into the Twilight Zone

Many people claim to have experienced some form of paranormal phenomenon, such as seeing a ghost, having a dream that predicted the future, or thinking about a friend moments before they telephone. These experiences have been debated throughout history and psychologists (myself included) have carried out research that has contributed to these discussions.

One strand of this work has examined the possible existence of extrasensory perception (the ability to psychically gain information from another person, a remote source, or a future event). Early work in the field often involved testing people who claimed strong extrasensory abilities, such as professional psychics and mediums. However, this work proved problematic because many of these individuals were exposed as frauds. As a result, most modern-day studies involve members of the public who do not claim to be psychic. Nevertheless, this work remains highly controversial, with proponents and sceptics frequently arguing about a wide range of methodological and statistical issues. One of the most recent, and significant, debates has centred on the work of Daryl Bem.

In 2011, Bem reported nine experiments that suggested that people could see into the future.[1] In one of his most successful studies, participants were presented with a long list of words, and then given a surprise recall test in which they were asked to remember as many of the words as possible. Next, the researchers randomly chose half of the words from the original list and showed them to the participants a second time. Bem's results seemed to suggest that seeing this second list of words influenced participants' earlier memories, because during the recall test, participants had recalled more of the words that they later saw at the end of the experiment. I teamed up with Chris French and Stuart Ritchie, and we each attempted to replicate this study.[2] Unlike the original studies reported by Bem, however, none of our experiments showed any evidence of extrasensory perception.

In contrast, some psychologists attempted to replicate some of Bem's studies and obtained positive outcomes.[3] Around the same time, researchers began to criticize Bem's research on various methodological and statistical grounds.[4] Bem and others eventually decided to help settle the issue by carrying out several large-scale studies into the alleged phenomenon.[5] These studies did not contain many of the potential issues associated with the initial studies, but also obtained null results and so didn't support the existence of extrasensory perception. Over the years, sceptics have argued that research into alleged paranormal phenomena has frequently exhibited the same pattern, with initial studies yielding positive outcomes but these findings proving difficult to replicate under more controlled conditions. Proponents of the work have argued against this notion.[6]

The debates around Bem's work had an unexpected impact on modern-day psychology. When his studies were first criticized, some researchers noted that the same types of flaws were also present in some mainstream psychological experiments. For example, to help prevent possible bias, researchers are supposed to decide how to analyse their data before they begin an experiment and then stick to that plan. However, critics argued that some researchers decided which statistical tests to conduct after looking at their data, and that this was biasing the outcome of their experiments. As a result, researchers were encouraged to formally pre-register their planned analyses prior to carrying out a study. Partly because of the Bem controversy, pre-registration is now more common within psychology and is helping to increase the quality of research.

This is not the only time that research into psychic ability has benefited mainstream psychology. For instance, around the turn of the last century, German scientist Hans Berger became fascinated by the idea of telepathy and tried to build a machine that could detect thoughts leaving the human mind. After many years of hard work, Berger eventually figured out how to monitor people's brain activity by placing several sensors on their scalp. He never demonstrated the existence of mind-to-mind contact, but his remarkable technique (known as electroencephalography, or 'EEG' for short) has proved to be vitally important in both science and medicine.

People have argued about seemingly paranormal experiences for centuries. Psychologists have made an important contribution to this debate by studying alleged psychic ability. In my opinion, this work does not support the existence of extrasensory perception, but it has nevertheless made a surprising and important contribution to mainstream science and psychology.

Informing and Resolving Debate

Who Do You Think You Are?

Over the years, many great thinkers have argued about how best to view the fundamental nature of humanity, and psychologists have contributed to this debate by developing and testing several different models of the mind. Each of these approaches has affected the nature of psychology by influencing the types of topics that researchers investigate and the way in which they conduct their studies. Perhaps most important of all, these different models of the mind have also changed the way in which people view themselves and others, and helped to shape key aspects of society, including educational and social policies, civil rights, law enforcement, and approaches to mental health issues. In this section, we are going to take a brief look at the seven main perspectives developed by psychologists.

First, the biological perspective examines how experiences and behaviour can be explained by studying brain activity, genetics, hormones, and so on. Work in this area might, for instance, involve using scanning techniques to identify which parts of the brain are especially active when people carry out certain mental tasks, investigate the degree to which certain psychological traits are inherited, or examine how hormones affect emotion. Seen from this perspective, you are your brain and body.

Second, the psychodynamic perspective focuses on how the unconscious mind influences thoughts, feelings, and behaviour. Sigmund Freud carried out pioneering work into this approach, including research that attempted to identify key components of the mind (which he referred to as the 'ego', 'id', and 'superego') and explored how childhood events shape adult lives. Freud also played a pivotal role in creating a type of talking therapy known as psychoanalysis. Modern-day psychodynamic thinking has evolved away from Freud's original ideas but continues to emphasize how your unconscious mind shapes your experiences and sense of self.

Third, there is behaviourism. In the late nineteenth century, Ivan Pavlov conducted a series of now famous studies in which he rang a bell whilst presenting dogs with food, and discovered that the dogs eventually salivated to the sound of the bell alone. This work showed that the dogs' behaviour could be shaped by external stimuli. A few years later, psychologists began to apply this approach to humans. Rather than studying minds, they focused on how behaviour was the result of reward and punishment. According to this approach, you are much like a robot responding to your surroundings in a predictable way.

Fourth, the cognitive perspective emerged, in part, as a reaction to behaviourism and shifted the spotlight onto internal mental processes. Cognitive psychologists examine how people process information, and how this can help to explain a range of phenomena, including perception, learning, attention, problem solving, decision making, memory, speech, and reading. Seen from this perspective, your mind is analogous to a computer that is inputting, processing, and outputting data.

Fifth, the sociocultural approach focuses on the power of situations and culture. Social psychologists examine a wide range of topics, including how people interact with others, conform to societal norms, create social identities, behave in groups, become aggressive, exhibit prejudice, and help one another. More broadly, the approach explores how cultural factors impact on people's thinking and behaviour, and encourages researchers to recognize the importance of diversity and culture in their work. Seen from this perspective, you are a product of your surroundings and culture.

Sixth, evolutionary psychology focuses on how thinking and behaviour have developed through natural selection, and have helped humanity to survive and reproduce. This work examines how evolutionary processes may yield insights into a range of phenomena, including sexual attraction and mating, sharing and co-operation, facial perception, emotion, language acquisition, and the ability to distinguish kin from non-kin. This approach sees you as a product of your evolutionary past.

Finally, there is the humanistic approach. Whereas most of the other perspectives adopt a nomothetic view of humans (i.e. they attempt to find universal rules that apply to most people), this approach argues that each person is unique and develops over time. This perspective emerged in the 1950s, is associated with the pioneering work of Carl Rogers and Abraham Maslow, and emphasizes personal autonomy, wellbeing, happiness, and self-actualization. According to the humanistic approach, you are unique, have the potential to grow, and possess the free will to choose your own path through life.

There's a well-known story in which three people are blindfolded, led into a room that contains an elephant, and asked to figure out what is in front of them. One person feels the elephant's trunk and believes that the room contains a snake. Another touches the elephant's leg and argues that they are surrounded by tree trunks. The final person places their hand on the tail of the elephant and thinks that it is a rope. In my opinion, the same applies to the various models of the mind. No single approach represents a complete and comprehensive account of what it is to be human. Rather, each perspective embodies part of a larger truth. Sometimes our behaviour is the result of our evolutionary past and other times it is due to our surroundings. Sometimes we are driven by our unconscious mind and other times by past rewards. Sometimes our thinking is influenced by our hormones and other times by our emotions. It is only by understanding this variety of approaches that we can gain a more rounded and accurate view of who we really are.

Perchance to Dream

Throughout history, people have speculated about why we dream. In Ancient Greece, it was widely believed that dreams contained important messages from the Gods, or were the result of the soul leaving the body, or represented an act of prophecy. Around the turn of the twentieth century, Sigmund Freud argued that people's dreams reflected their unconscious wishes and desires, and could therefore act as a valuable source of information within a therapeutic context. More recent psychological research has uncovered several important insights into the dreaming mind.

From the 1950s onwards, researchers began connecting people to EEG machines and monitoring their brain activity throughout the night. At several points during the sleep cycle, participants' brain activity suddenly increased, and their eyes darted from side to side. This state became known as Rapid Eye Movement sleep (or REM sleep for short). Moreover, if participants were woken up during, or directly after, REM sleep, they were highly likely to report a dream. Over the years, scientists have employed this technique to discover several important insights into dreaming, including the fact that most dreams reflect events that are happening in people's everyday lives and that many dreams involve some form of negative emotion. In addition, researchers also began to explore some of the psychological processes associated with dreaming.

Several artists, writers, and scientists have described having creative ideas in their dreams. For instance, the plot for *The Strange Case of Dr Jekyll and Mr Hyde* came to Robert Louis Stevenson whilst he was dreaming, and Mary Shelley was similarly inspired to create her novel *Frankenstein*.

In addition, chemist Dmitri Mendeleev created the modern-day periodic table after a dream and August Kekulé discovered the ring-like structure of benzene after dreaming about a snake biting its own tail. Intrigued by these experiences, researchers began to conduct studies that explored the possible link between creativity and dreaming.

In one study, Matthew Walker and colleagues invited volunteers into a sleep laboratory and woke them up several times during the night.[7] Each time, the participants were asked to try to solve several anagrams (e.g. they might have to rearrange the letters TSOBO into the word BOOST). Sometimes the participants were woken up from non-REM sleep and other times they were disturbed when they were in REM sleep. When they were woken up during non-REM sleep, they only solved a handful of the anagrams. However, when they were woken up during REM sleep, they solved far more of the puzzles, with many of the participants reporting that the answers just seemed to pop into their mind.

Other research suggests that coming up with creative ideas during dreaming may help people to solve important issues in their lives. Harvard sleep expert Deidre Barrett carried out studies in which people facing key life decisions (such as a change in their career or relationship) have benefited from the insights and possible solutions that have emerged in their dreams.[8] Similarly, psychotherapist Clara Hill and colleagues have explored how dream work helps people to deal with a wide range of psychological issues, including low self-esteem, difficult relationships, and depression.[9] More recently, Michael Olsen surveyed over 600 participants about how their dreams had affected their lives.[10] Just over 60% of participants indicated that they had had a 'helpful' dream, with many describing how the experience had helped to inform key life decisions.

For thousands of years, scholars have speculated about the nature of dreaming. It is likely that this strange state of consciousness serves many purposes. However, a large body of psychological research now suggests that dreaming plays an important role in creative thinking and can help people to find innovative solutions to important issues.

Shocking Science

Academics and writers have long debated why some people are prepared to kill and injure others. Do we all have the potential to act in this way or is such behaviour the preserve of those with especially cruel dispositions? In the 1960s, Stanley Milgram made a substantial contribution to this debate by conducting a series of highly controversial studies that have since featured in almost every textbook on psychology.

Milgram devised the studies and secretly observed many of the sessions through a one-way mirror. In a typical experiment, participants were told that they would be taking part in a study about the effects of punishment on learning. When they arrived at the laboratory, an experimenter introduced them to someone who appeared to be another volunteer. In fact, this apparent volunteer was an actor working for the research team. Next, the genuine participant and actor were assigned to the roles of 'teacher' and 'learner' respectively. The two of them were placed into separate rooms but could hear one another, and the experimenter asked the teacher to read out several word pairs for the learner to memorize (e.g. dog–curtains). The teacher was then instructed to read out the first word of each pair and the learner was required to try to recall the second word. If the learner made a mistake, the teacher was asked to punish them by pressing a button that apparently administered an electric shock. The markings on the shock machine suggested that the intensity of the shocks was increasing as the study continued. In fact, there were no electric shocks, and the learner was acting out a pre-arranged script. After the first few 'shocks', the learner began to scream. As the experiment progressed, the learner mentioned a problem with their heart and eventually refused to continue. Despite being met by silence from the learner, the experimenter urged the teacher to continue administering the ever-increasing shocks.

Milgram carried out many versions of the experiment. In the best-known of these studies, around 65% of participants were prepared to inflict the maximum intensity of shock on the learner, despite the buttons on the apparatus being labelled 'Danger: Severe Shock' and 'XXX'. Milgram argued that these findings showed that a surprisingly large number of people are prepared to inflict significant pain on others if ordered to do so by an authority figure.

Perhaps not surprisingly, Milgram's shock study has attracted a considerable amount of controversy over the years. Some of the commentary questioned the ethical aspects of the work and this eventually led to the development of guidelines that aim to prevent participants experiencing serious distress during psychology experiments. Other criticism focused on Milgram's methodology. For instance, Gina Perry studied his original research material, and argued that some of the volunteers didn't believe that the experimental setup was genuine and therefore knew that they weren't really delivering harmful electric shocks.[11] In addition, Perry has noted that although Milgram said that the experimenter used four verbal prompts to urge the teacher to continue (such as 'Please continue' and 'It is absolutely essential that you continue'), they frequently exerted far more pressure.

Proponents of the study note that many versions of Milgram's studies have been conducted over the years and have often obtained broadly similar findings.[12] Although this work has involved a relatively small number of participants, it has been conducted in many different countries and cultures, including Italy, Germany, Jordan, South Africa, and Australia. One of the most dramatic re-creations took place on French television and involved participants who thought that they were taking part in a game show.[13] Encouraged by a presenter and the studio audience, 80% of participants delivered an electric shock that, if genuine, would have been potentially lethal.

Some researchers believe that Milgram's results reflect a genuine effect but don't agree with the way in which he interpreted his findings. Milgram argued that the participants seemed to enter an 'agentic state' in which they focused on obeying authority to such an extent that they became unaware of their actions. In contrast, Stephen Reicher and colleagues have proposed that the participants administered the shocks because they identified with the experimenter and believed that they were contributing to a greater good, such as the advancement of science.[14] In support of this latter position, Stephen Gibson carried out a qualitative analysis of Milgram's audio recordings and transcripts, and concluded that the experimenter was *least* effective at obtaining obedience when they ordered the participant to continue.[15]

Milgram's studies have generated a vast amount of debate about several important topics, including whether good people can be persuaded to harm others, the degree to which we obey authority figures, and the ethical boundaries of psychological research. As Milgram's biographer Thomas Blass noted, regardless of the outcome of these debates, there is little doubt that his studies shocked the world.[16]

Informing and Resolving Debate

In Two Minds

In the 1960s, American surgeons developed a novel way of treating epilepsy.[17] The brain consists of two hemispheres that are connected to one another by a series of nerve fibres known as the corpus callosum. During some epileptic fits, excessive brain activity quickly spreads from one hemisphere to the other, and the surgeons wondered if cutting the corpus callosum might help to prevent this issue. They operated on several patients with considerable success.

Michael Gazzaniga and Roger Sperry wondered whether these so-called 'split-brain' individuals might help to reveal unique insights into the mystery of consciousness. To appreciate their remarkable experiments, we first need to understand the relationship between each hemisphere of the brain and each side of the body. In general, the right hemisphere receives images from the left side of the visual field and controls the left side of the body. Similarly, the left hemisphere receives information from the right side of the visual field and controls the right side of the body. Normally, this visual information and bodily control quickly moves between the hemispheres via the corpus callosum and so involves both sides of the brain. However, in split-brain individuals, the lack of a corpus callosum prevents such sharing. In some studies, participants were asked to look at a dot in the middle of a screen whilst researchers flashed up a picture either side of the dot. When the researchers flashed a picture of an object to the right of the dot, the information flowed to the participant's left hemisphere. As most people's speech centre is in the left hemisphere, it's not surprising that they then reported seeing the picture. However, when the same picture was flashed up to the left of the dot, the information went to the participant's right hemisphere and they said that they hadn't seen anything. On the face of it, these results suggested that the participant was not consciously aware of the image. This was, however, far from the full story.

In another set of studies, the researchers again flashed up a picture to the left of the dot and again the participants denied seeing anything. However, this time, the researchers presented the participant with several objects and asked them to point to any one of the objects with their left hand. Although the participants felt like they were pointing randomly, they frequently selected the object that had been flashed up to the left of the dot. For instance, the word APPLE might be flashed up on the left side of the screen, and then the participant would be shown various objects and asked to point to one of them with their left hand. The participant would say that they didn't see an image on the screen but nevertheless point to the apple. In one particularly dramatic version of this effect, a participant was shown the word TEXAS on the left side of the screen, denied seeing anything, and was then asked to make any drawing with his left hand. Remarkably, he drew a picture of a cowboy hat. Interestingly, when asked to account for their choices and drawings, the participants often tried to explain away their actions, describing, for instance, how they just like apples or cowboy hats.

The findings raise fascinating questions about the nature of consciousness. Some researchers have argued that splitting the brain essentially created two separate conscious agents. The 'person' in the left hemisphere was able to speak and dominate the participant's sense of self, whilst the 'person' in the right hemisphere couldn't speak but nevertheless performed relatively complex tasks, such as picture recognition and drawing. This interpretation raises a series of fascinating philosophical questions. For instance, is the 'person' in the right hemisphere conscious? If so, who are they and do they exist in people who have not had their corpus callosum cut?

Informing and Resolving Debate

Over the years, this work has attracted a considerable amount of debate.[18] Recently, some researchers have re-tested some split-brain patients and argued that their results do not support the idea of a divided consciousness. In reply, opponents have suggested that the original interpretation holds, and that these new findings might be due to information travelling between the two hemispheres via other brain structures or one side of the body subtly cueing the other. Ongoing research is tackling these issues and the work provides a compelling illustration of how psychology can provide important insight into the mysteries of consciousness.

The Power of Mindsets

Educational psychologists frequently study why some children struggle at school and what can be done to help them flourish. There are many factors at work, including classroom size, availability of educational resources, attitudes towards learning, teacher training, and the child's socioeconomic status and family life. One of the most widely debated approaches has been pioneered by Carol Dweck and focuses on the way in which children view their abilities, skills, and intelligence.[19]

According to Dweck's theory, children possess one of two general mindsets. Those with a so-called *fixed mindset* assume that their abilities and skills are set in stone and so do not change over time. In contrast, those with a *growth mindset* assume that their abilities are far more malleable and are modified by effort and experience. Several studies have assessed how these different mindsets impact on children's academic performance. In one study, for instance, Lisa Blackwell and colleagues spent several years tracking school children as they studied mathematics.[20] Those with a growth mindset started to achieve higher marks than those with a fixed mindset, and by the end of the course they had obtained significantly better grades. Eager to discover what explained this intriguing effect, the researchers explored how the children's mindsets had impacted on their studies. They discovered that children with a growth mindset thought that they could develop and change, and reported being far more open to tackling challenging mathematical problems and learning from their mistakes.

In a second study, the researchers examined the academic impact of encouraging children to develop a growth mindset. During the experiment, one group of children attended a short course that was designed to highlight how their intelligence and abilities are malleable. In contrast, another group of students acted as a control, and received general lessons on memory and studying. Whilst the academic performance of those in the control group declined over time, the grades of the children who were encouraged to develop a growth mindset increased.

Other work has shown that it can be relatively straightforward to encourage a growth mindset. In a study conducted by Claudia Mueller and Carol Dweck, one group of children were commended for their natural intelligence ('You are bright') whilst another group received praise for their effort ('You must have worked hard'). Those in the latter group tended to cultivate a growth mindset and, as a result, were more likely to work harder and persist in the face of failure.[21]

More recently, several researchers have been involved in debates and discussions about Dweck's theory.

Some of this work has focused on replicating key effects. For instance, in a series of studies conducted with Chinese children, Yue Li and Timothy Bates reported that they were unable to replicate the impact of praising effort over natural ability.[22] However, Carol Dweck and David Yeager have criticized the methodology and statistics of these studies, and argued that many of the findings support the mindset theory.[23] Other work by Victoria Sisk and colleagues involved collecting lots of studies that have investigated mindsets and analysing them en masse (an approach known as meta-analysis).[24] Some of this work examined the relationship between growth mindset and academic performance, and other work investigated the effects of interventions designed to promote a growth mindset. The authors argued that the findings suggested a weak relationship between mindsets and academic achievement and that the interventions only had a small overall effect. They also noted that students who had low socioeconomic status, and those who were academically at risk, benefited from developing a growth mindset. Again, other researchers have been critical of this work, noting, for instance, that some of these effects are impressive when viewed within the context of other educational interventions.[25] Additional work has involved carrying out large-scale studies into the impact of growth mindsets and obtained positive results. For instance, one international study involved over half a million students drawn from seventy-four countries and showed that a growth mindset was positively related to academic performance in almost all of the nations.[26]

A second strand of debate has revolved around the circumstances and contexts in which such mindsets are especially effective. For instance, David Yeager and colleagues evaluated the effect of online programmes that were designed to encourage a growth mindset.[27] More than 12,000 students from American public schools participated and the findings revealed that the intervention led to higher grades for lower-achieving students, and that this was especially the case in schools that had a culture of celebrating academic success and fostering curiosity. Other work by Yeager has shown that teachers' mindsets also influence their students' mindset and academic attainment.[28] This work is essential to understanding how to create interventions that are maximally effective.

In short, much of the early research into Dweck's theory about mindsets yielded positive results and the idea was quickly incorporated into classrooms across the world. This work has attracted considerable attention, with much of the more recent research in this area focusing on replicating key effects and identifying how best to encourage growth mindsets.

Why Psychology Matters: Informing and Resolving Debate

In this chapter, we have seen how psychologists have helped to sharpen and shape important debates, including work that has explored the existence of psychic ability, influenced the way in which we see ourselves, uncovered the mysteries of dreaming, examined why people are prepared to harm others, yielded valuable insights into consciousness, and investigated how to boost children's academic performance. Together, this important body of work illustrates another key reason why psychology matters.

5

Creating a Better World

A great deal of psychological research aims to make the world a better place. Some of this work focuses on enriching the lives of individuals by helping them to become happier, to gain qualifications, to build better relationships, to cope with mental health issues, to adopt a healthier lifestyle, and much more. Other work aims to improve communities and society by reducing prejudice and injustice, promoting altruism and equality, enhancing educational opportunities, informing positive social and political policies, preventing homelessness, and encouraging sustainability. In this chapter, we will explore several projects that illustrate the remarkable diversity of this work.

Exploring Mental Health Issues

Imagine standing on the bank of a fast-flowing river and suddenly seeing a person being swept along by the current. The person appears to be drowning and they are shouting for help. Being a good citizen and a strong swimmer, you quickly jump into the water and pull the person to safety. However, moments later you see a second person being swept along and they are also in need of assistance. Once again, you jump into the river and manage to get them safely to the bank. Next, a third person appears in the river, and again you save them. And so it goes on. There are two main approaches to preventing people from drowning. One approach involves going upstream and preventing people from falling into the river in the first place. Alternatively, you can remain downstream and find ways of pulling people to safety. Similarly, research into mental health issues involves both upstream and downstream approaches.[1]

Researchers taking an upstream approach focus on how poor mental health is associated with various societal issues, including poverty, inadequate housing provision, racism, bad working conditions, a lack of educational opportunities, and unemployment. Some of this work is carried out by community psychologists and will be discussed later in this chapter.

Downstream work takes a more person-centred view of mental health issues. In Chapter 3, we explored the main paradigms created by researchers to understand the human mind (e.g. psychodynamic, cognitive, evolutionary, humanistic). These perspectives also influence how psychologists view mental health issues and the types of support that they develop. For instance, researchers adopting the biomedical perspective might examine how such issues are related to the structure and functioning of the brain, and try to develop effective forms of medication. In contrast, those interested in the psychodynamic approach are more likely to explore whether some mental health issues are the result of certain life events (e.g. childhood experiences and past relationships), and favour psychotherapy that involves therapists and clients exploring these issues in depth. Humanist practitioners employ a range of techniques, including, for example, the person-centred approach, in which therapists treat each client as unique, and there is a focus on setting goals that are designed to help them to flourish. The behavioural approach usually focuses on changing people's response to certain events and objects. For instance, a person with a phobia might be encouraged to carry out a relaxation exercise whilst experiencing whatever it is that makes them feel anxious. Finally, the cognitive approach examines whether certain mental health issues are related to people's thoughts and beliefs, and whether it helps to replace such thinking with more positive alternatives. For example, a person who believes that they will never have a successful career might be encouraged to engage in self-talk that confronts and minimizes their negative thinking. Although these perspectives are theoretically very different from one another, practitioners often employ them in combination.

A large amount of research has attempted to assess the efficacy of such support. These studies often prove contentious, but many of the researchers involved in this work argue that, in general, individuals not undergoing any support tend to improve, but that some forms of therapy and medication significantly increase the chance and speed of such improvements. This work also suggests that, in general, therapies are often most effective when they provide hope, offer new perspectives, and involve an empathic and trusting relationship between the client and therapist. Some of the most recent work in the area examines how the culture and background of researchers, practitioners, and clients impact on key topics, including the perception of mental health issues, access to healthcare systems, and the perception and delivery of support.

MAGIC WORDS

Health psychologists examine a range of issues, including why some people fail to adhere to medical advice, techniques for enhancing pain control, and ways of changing unhealthy habits.

One strand of this work aims to enhance people's engagement with health systems. For instance, research conducted by John Heritage and colleagues aimed to encourage patients to mention additional health issues at the end of a consultation. In everyday conversation, the word 'any' often appears in a negative context ('I haven't got any money') whereas the word 'some' is more positive ('I've got some money'). The researchers wondered whether this linguistic quirk could be put to good use in a medical context. During the study, some doctors were asked to end their consultations by asking 'Is there *anything* else you want to talk about today?' whilst others said, 'Is there *something* else you want to talk about today?' As predicted, patients in the latter group were far more likely to mention additional medical concerns.

Similar work by Hengchen Dai and colleagues recently examined whether small changes in the wording of reminder messages can encourage people to be vaccinated. In one study, over 90,000 people in an American health system were contacted by text, and either received a regular reminder or a message that encouraged a sense of ownership by including the phrase 'claim your dose'. This small change in wording had a considerable impact and boosted the number of people attending their appointment. This effect was not significantly affected by participants' ethnicity or age, but further studies aim to examine whether the messaging is equally effective in other contexts and cultures.

Sources: J. Heritage, J.D. Robinson, M.N. Elliott, M. Beckett, & M. Wilkes, 'Reducing patients' unmet concerns in primary care: The difference one word can make', *Journal of General Internal Medicine*, 22(10) (2007), 1429–1433; H. Dai, S. Saccardo, M.A. Han, *et al.*, 'Behavioural nudges increase COVID-19 vaccinations', *Nature*, 597 (2021), 404–409.

All Together Now

Community psychology examines how a range of social factors negatively impact on people's wellbeing and often aims to develop multi-level interventions that help to tackle these issues. This approach embraces several key principles, including valuing diversity and lived experience, encouraging active participation by citizens, employing both quantitative and qualitative research methods, and empowering groups and communities.

In one early example of this work, American psychologist George Fairweather employed a community-based approach to help patients who were struggling after spending time in psychiatric facilities.[2] This work was initiated in the 1960s and involved a co-created space in which individuals shared responsibilities, supported each other, and formed a meaningful community. The system was managed through joint decision making with staff acting as advisers.

In a more recent example, Sally Zlotowitz and colleagues tackled serious youth violence on an inner-city housing estate.[3] Young people's involvement in violence is often associated with several factors, including mental health issues, low employment opportunities, and a lack of social support. During the project, researchers, practitioners, and young people worked together to create music-based activities (such as DJing) that helped to build relationships and facilitate discussions around these issues. At one point, they staged a workshop about how to be successful in the music industry and used this opportunity to examine the role of self-confidence, and the benefits of avoiding drug use and building positive relationships. Other aspects of the project involved working with the young people to identify key needs and then helping them to access relevant support. This work tackled several issues, including making benefit applications and finding employment. There was also an emphasis on supporting youth-led projects that helped to address community and social issues that impact marginalized young people. The project was evaluated by interviewing the individuals involved and then looking for key themes within these discussions. This qualitative approach revealed six important themes, including the notion that building a trusted relationship with practitioners facilitated communication, and that co-creating the music-based activities encouraged more positive interactions than traditional forms of intervention. This approach has since been employed with several other communities.

Other work in this area involves assessing the effect of legal and social policies on communities. In one study, for instance, Leonard Jason examined the impact of new anti-smoking legislation in a suburban community of Chicago.[4] The regulations were designed to curb the sale of cigarettes to minors and involved vendors receiving a hefty fine for illegally selling tobacco. After collecting observational data for a year and a half, Jason and colleagues discovered that the new legislation, along with quarterly police checks to ensure that they were being adhered to, significantly reduced the sale of cigarettes to minors. In addition, a survey of students at a junior high school revealed that their regular use of cigarettes had fallen by over 50%.

Community psychology recognizes the interconnectedness of individuals and society and presents ecologically orientated theories and solutions. This approach has helped to develop and assess interventions that are innovative, positive, inclusive, and effective.

DISCOVERING DYSLEXIA

Dyslexia is often characterized by difficulties with word recognition, spelling, writing, and vocabulary. More positively, it's also frequently associated with greater creativity and enhanced lateral thinking. Some qualitative work in the area has explored the lived experiences of those with dyslexia. For instance, in one study, Lois MacCullagh and colleagues examined the learning experience of students with dyslexia at university.

The study was carried out by a dyslexic researcher and other experts, and involved interviewing both students with and without dyslexia about a variety of learning-related topics. Several key themes emerged. For instance, some of the students with dyslexia found it especially difficult to listen to their tutors and to take notes simultaneously, and frequently remarked upon the importance of lecturers recording their talks, in order that they could listen to the live lecture and then make notes from the recording. They also described creating more visually orientated notes, including those containing flow diagrams, pictures, and charts. Interestingly, the additional effort associated with these procedures appeared to encourage deeper engagement and enhanced learning. In another part of the interviews, the students with dyslexia commented on the limitations of receiving extra time in exams, noting that the adjustment wasn't especially helpful if the initial part of the exam had made them feel tired.

As is often the case with qualitative work, this study provided a detailed description of participants' lived experiences, and resulted in useful insights that can improve lives.

Source: L. MacCullagh, A. Bosanquet, & N.A. Badcock, 'University students with dyslexia: A qualitative exploratory study of learning practices, challenges and strategies', *Dyslexia*, 23(1) (2017), 3–23.

Creating a Better World

Tackling Prejudice

A vast amount of research has explored the psychology of prejudice and discrimination. One significant strand of this research has examined the relationship between racism and health.[5] In America, the results from several surveys suggest that the stress of experiencing racism is associated with a weakened immune system and poor physical wellbeing. These findings are supported by a significant amount of laboratory work. For instance, in a series of studies, Jules P. Harrell and colleagues monitored the physiology of African American participants as they imagined racist events or watched films depicting racism.[6] The participants exhibited increased cardiovascular activity and elevated blood pressure, both of which are strongly related to long-term poor health outcomes. Related work has shown that experiencing racial discrimination is also strongly associated with behaviours that have a negative impact on health, including an increased risk of smoking, alcohol intake, and poor sleep. Other research suggests that these effects are exacerbated by poor access to healthcare and undertreatment.[7]

A similar picture emerges when it comes to psychological health, with many surveys suggesting that experiencing racism is associated with an increased risk of several mental health issues, including depression, anxiety, and post-traumatic stress disorder. Some recent work in this area has examined the relationship between racism and mental health among different groups of individuals. For example, Briana Brownlow and colleagues reviewed studies that examined how African American men and women employ different coping strategies to deal with racial discrimination, and how these differences impact on their mental health.[8] This review suggested, for instance, that whilst some coping strategies (e.g. emotional eating) were employed by both men and women, others (e.g. turning to religion and seeking social support) were more commonly used by women than men.

Other work on the psychology of prejudice has aimed to develop interventions that reduce discrimination in schools, workplaces, and communities. Some of this work has involved creating effective training programmes, noting the existence of implicit biases, and shaping media messaging. One of the most researched areas explores whether it's possible to reduce discrimination in schools by promoting contact between members of different groups. For instance, Elliot Aronson developed a form of co-operative learning known as 'The Jigsaw Method'. The first step involves dividing the topic being studied into several small segments. The class is then split into small, diverse, groups, and each member of each group is asked to learn about one of the segments. Next, the pupils who have investigated the same segment come together and discuss their work. Everyone then returns to their original groupings and each pupil explains what they have learnt to their group. Finally, all the pupils are tested on all the segments. Another technique involves encouraging children to make friends with classmates from different cultural and ethnic backgrounds by exploring shared interests and hobbies. Research suggests that these approaches help to reduce children's stereotypical opinions of one another, and that these positive effects are maintained into adulthood.[9]

LONG COVID

Caitriona Callan and colleagues recently carried out a large-scale qualitative study exploring the lived experience of people with long COVID. This UK-based study was conducted with the help of people with long COVID, and involved interviews with fifty participants who spanned a range of ages and ethnic and social backgrounds. The interviews revealed that the participants experienced various psychological issues, including poor decision making, memory disruption, and difficulties in sustaining attention. These factors, combined with physical fatigue, had a profound negative impact on many aspects of participants' personal and professional lives, including their relationships, work, and self-identity. In addition, access to the healthcare system often proved challenging for them because it required psychological skills that they now lacked. Participants also reported feeling frustrated and angry when healthcare professionals dismissed the impact of long COVID, but they reported a sense of relief when their symptoms were acknowledged. This work could help to develop healthcare systems that are more accessible to those with long COVID, and to encourage some practitioners to better support such individuals.

Source: C. Callan, E. Ladds, L. Husain, K. Pattinson, & T. Greenhalgh, '"I can't cope with multiple inputs": Qualitative study of the lived experience of "brain fog" after COVID-19', *BMJ Open*, 12(2) (2022), https://bmjopen.bmj.com/content/12/2/e056366.info.

Find Me

Severe brain injury or trauma can result in a neurological condition known as Unresponsive Wakefulness Syndrome (or UWS for short). Those diagnosed with the syndrome aren't aware of themselves or their surroundings. At times, their eyes may open, or they might smile or yawn. Although these actions can give the impression that such individuals are conscious, the movements are not under their voluntary control and are more akin to reflexes. Accurately diagnosing UWS is challenging. It's possible that an individual is conscious, but cannot control their movements and so has no way of communicating with the outside world. If this is the case, they run the risk of being misdiagnosed with UWS when in fact they are self-aware and locked inside their bodies. As a result, researchers and practitioners have frequently discussed how best to differentiate these two different conditions. Adrian Owen and colleagues have carried out pioneering work into this issue.

Unlike many of the researchers mentioned in this book, I know Adrian personally. We first crossed paths as psychology undergraduates, shared a flat, and even performed together in a magic act. Adrian has spent much of his career investigating a technique known as functional magnetic resonance imaging (or fMRI for short), which involves placing a powerful (but harmless) magnetic field across a person's brain whilst they carry out various mental tasks. The resulting data allow researchers to detect changes in blood flow around the brain, and therefore identify which parts of the brain appear to be especially active during the task.

In the late 1990s, Adrian and colleagues were using a similar (but less sophisticated) scanning technique to examine which parts of a person's brain become especially active when they see a face that they recognize. At one point, they arranged for a young woman who had been diagnosed with UWS to be scanned and discovered that the regions in her brain associated with facial recognition became active when she was presented with a familiar face. As a result, they suspected that she might be aware but locked in. Their conclusions turned out to be correct. The woman responded well to rehabilitation and several years later thanked the team for their remarkable work.

In 2006, Adrian arranged for another patient with UWS to be placed into an fMRI scanner, and asked her to do things: to imagine playing tennis and think about walking through her house. When a healthy person imagines playing tennis, an area towards the top of their brain (known as the premotor cortex) becomes especially activated, whereas when they think about walking through their house, the activity is more focused towards an area in the middle of the brain (known as the parahippocampal gyrus).

The patient showed the same type of brain activation patterns, and so the research team suspected that she might be conscious but locked in. Adrian then repeated the procedure on around fifty patients diagnosed with UWS, and believed that around one in five appeared to be aware and locked in. Encouraged by these findings, he even used the technique to have another patient answer six questions about their life. After each question, the patient was asked to imagine playing tennis if the answer was 'yes' and think about walking through their house to indicate 'no'. Focusing on simple questions, such as his father's name, the patient answered five of six questions correctly.

Thousands of people across the world are diagnosed with UWS each year, and this technique offers the chance of identifying those who may be locked in. Potentially, it could also help to provide an insight into their otherwise hidden experiences, and so contribute to debates about consciousness, self-awareness, and the nature of identity. The next stage of the work aims to develop an EEG-based version of the procedure in order that it can be more readily used by clinicians and family members. If this can be achieved, it has the potential to inform treatments such as pain management and rehabilitation resources. The technique raises several fascinating ethical issues, but also shows how psychology and neuroscience can help to improve lives.

Positive Psychology

Positive psychologists carry out research into what makes life worth living. This idea has a long history within psychology (including the work of humanist psychologists Abraham Maslow and Carl Rogers), but became especially popular in the 1990s when researchers such as Martin Seligman and Mihaly Csikszentmihalyi stressed the need for the discipline to move away from what they perceived as an over-emphasis on illness.

One significant strand of this work aims to identify the factors that underpin happiness. Take, for example, the research into the psychology of gratitude. Let's imagine that you love the smell of freshly ground coffee and therefore enjoy going into your local café. However, you may have noticed that if you remain in the café for any length of time, you get used to the smell and no longer notice it. This 'habituation' effect is due to your perceptual systems tending to respond to change. To experience the smell of coffee again, you would have to leave the café, wait a while, and then return. The same idea applies to many aspects of our lives. We often habituate to whatever it is that makes us happy (such as our friends, family, health) and, after a while, stop noticing them. Robert Emmons and Michael McCullough wondered whether it was possible to increase people's happiness by encouraging them to remember and value these elements.[10] In one of their studies, one group of participants were asked to spend a few moments each week jotting down a few things in their lives for which they were grateful, a second group had to describe things that annoyed them, and a final group wrote about events that had taken place throughout the week. Throughout the study, participants were asked to rate how happy and healthy they were. As expected, those expressing a sense of gratitude were reminded of the good things in their lives, and reported being significantly happier and physically healthier.

Another strand of positive psychology has involved helping people to identify their 'signature strengths' (positive personal characteristics that appear essential to who they are) and encouraging them to find new ways of utilizing these traits. Much of this research has involved participants completing the 'Values in Action Inventory of Strengths' (a questionnaire designed to identify key strengths, such as creativity, curiosity, bravery, honesty, kindness, etc.), and then finding novel ways of incorporating these traits into their personal and professional lives. This work has involved a diverse range of cohorts drawn from several countries, and suggests that the intervention results in several benefits, including increased happiness, enhanced work satisfaction, better relationships, and a decreased risk of depression.[11]

Other research in positive psychology has examined some of the factors that underpin a meaningful life, including having a sense of purpose, helping others, and contributing to a greater good. For instance, work carried out by Amy Wrzesniewski and colleagues has explored the effects of promoting meaningfulness in the workplace. In some of these studies, researchers have asked people to think about ways in which their jobs benefit others.[12] A teacher might, for example, contemplate how they improve pupils' lives, and a train driver might think about how they help travellers to spend valuable time with family and friends. This simple exercise significantly boosted participants' perceptions of meaningfulness and increased their sense of life satisfaction. Related work has examined the impact of being kind to others. For example, work by Sonja Lyubomirsky and her colleagues suggests that carrying out a few small acts of kindness each week (such as giving money to the homeless, donating blood, or helping a neighbour) significantly boosts wellbeing.[13]

Most recently, some researchers have suggested that a concept known as 'psychological richness' may also be vital to life satisfaction. This work emphasizes the important role played by novelty seeking, curiosity, and experiences that shift a person's view of themselves or the world. In one study, for instance, Shigehiro Oishi and colleagues asked students in both China and America to keep a diary of their experiences and to rate the psychological richness of their lives.[14] The results showed that taking short trips and studying abroad proved especially effective ways of enhancing richness. Interestingly, neither type of experience was consistently associated with a happy or meaningful life.

Positive psychology has made significant inroads towards understanding what makes life worth living. However, as with any area of psychology, it has been subject to critical scrutiny. For instance, some researchers have raised methodological concerns about certain studies and others have argued that the field tends to underplay the role that societal factors play in determining happiness.[15] In addition, much of this work has been carried out in America and with student cohorts. However, researchers have now started to explore the degree to which this work generalizes to other cultures and groups of individuals, and to develop theories and interventions within this more diverse context.[16]

Sustainability

As we discovered in Chapter 1, our beliefs and actions are frequently the result of bias and wishful thinking. When it comes to climate change, these factors can cause people to underestimate the scale of the problem, convince themselves that they will be able to avoid potential harm, and justify doing little to help alleviate the issue. As a result, simply providing people with the facts about climate change doesn't tend to result in significant behavioural shifts. Fortunately, psychologists have developed more effective ways of helping people and organizations to recognize the scale of the problem and to embrace sustainability.[17]

One approach involves framing the required changes as opportunities rather than losses.[18] For example, emphasizing the significant health benefits associated with walking helps to decrease car usage, and pointing out that plant-based diets are associated with a reduced risk of developing certain cancers encourages people to consume less red meat.

Other work is based upon the notion that people often conform to group norms. In one study, Noah Goldstein and colleagues used this approach to encourage hotel guests to reuse their bath towels.[19] The researchers placed one of two signs in almost 200 hotel rooms. One sign contained a standard environmental message (e.g. 'Help save the environment') whilst the other noted that many guests were reusing their bath towels (e.g. 'Join your fellow guests in helping to save the environment'). The latter sign resulted in significantly higher levels of bath towel reuse. Establishing sustainable behaviours as normative and desirable activities is likely to play a key role in motivating people to adopt these practices.

Another approach is based on studies suggesting that people pay attention to threats that are personal, relatable, and concrete. For instance, in an experiment conducted by Deborah Small and colleagues, some participants were shown statistics about child poverty whilst others were presented with a story about the tragic plight of just one young girl.[20] The participants were then given an opportunity to contribute to a charity fighting child poverty, and those who had been shown the story of the girl contributed significantly more than those who had been presented with the statistical information. The media often illustrate climate change with statistics and graphs about the erosion of rainforests and the melting of glaciers. Making the impact of climate change far more concrete, local, and personal is likely to prove a more effective approach.

Finally, much of the media messaging around climate change is fear-based and involves worst-case scenarios and apocalyptic predictions about the future. There is a risk that this approach makes people feel defensive, disempowered, and fatalistic. Some researchers have started to tackle this issue by exploring other forms of messaging. For instance, work by Chris Skurka and colleagues examined a more humour-based approach.[21] The researchers teamed up with professional comedians from Second City Chicago to create three videos in which a weather presenter delivered information about climate change. In one video, the material was presented in a serious and bleak way (fear), in a second video the presenter appeared incompetent and unable to account for the changes (humour), and in the third video the presentation was more straightforward and factual (informational). Young adults watched one of the videos and then completed several questionnaires concerning their thoughts about climate change. Humour turned out to be an especially effective way of inspiring younger participants (aged eighteen to twenty-five) to engage in climate-related personal activism and political action, whilst the fear-based messaging tended to raise awareness about the risks associated with climate change across all ages. Although many advertisements and public service announcements about climate change are fear-based, these findings suggest that there may also be a role to be played by somewhat more light-hearted messaging.

Climate change is one of the most pressing problems facing humanity and a wide range of psychologists are tackling the issue. Researchers interested in the perception of risk are looking at how best to help the public to develop a realistic understanding of the challenges. Behavioural change practitioners are developing interventions that encourage people to alter their lifestyle. Communication experts are helping to shape media messaging and public infor- mation campaigns. Organizational psychologists are helping businesses to change the way in which they go about their business. Political psychologists are helping to shape public policy and political narratives. It is a complex issue, but psychology is playing an important role in creating a brighter and more sustainable future.

Why Psychology Matters: Creating a Better World

In this chapter, we have seen how psychology can help to improve the lives of individuals and change society, including work that explores mental health issues, builds stronger communities, reduces prejudice, promotes physical wellbeing, increases happiness, and encourages sustainability. These examples are just the tip of the iceberg. In other work, organizational psychologists help to promote productivity and wellbeing in the workplace, forensic psychologists help to improve the justice system and reduce reoffending, educational psychologists help to promote learning and growth, sports psychologists help to encourage physical activity and boost athletic performance, traffic psychologists help to reduce road accidents, and much more. Together, this work has touched the lives of millions of people and helped to create a better world.

Conclusion

As I said at the very start of our journey, I do not believe that all psychology matters. Some research has been of very little interest to anyone, and other work has had a negative impact on individuals and society. However, during our time together, we have focused our attention on psychology at its best and uncovered five ways in which the discipline is vitally important. In this final chapter, we will explore why psychology is especially relevant right now and examine how to encourage even more meaningful research in the future.

We began in Chapter 1 by exploring how psychologists produce interesting, surprising, and counter-intuitive insights into the way in which people think, feel, and behave. The work described in this chapter often stemmed from a sense of curiosity and an openness to examine areas neglected by other researchers. For instance, John Darley and Bibb Latané's work into why people frequently fail to help others was motivated by media reports of an incident in which several people heard a woman being attacked but didn't come to her aid.[1] Similarly, Tony Cornell's early research into the observation of ghost-like phenomena was driven by his lifelong fascination with the paranormal. This sense of curiosity and openness has played a key role in several important discoveries throughout the history of psychology. For instance, perceptual psychologist Richard Gregory and his team once spotted a new optical illusion formed by some ceramic tiles outside their local coffee shop. Subsequent research into this illusion provided interesting insights into the visual system. James Laird once noticed that he felt happier when he forced his face into a smile, and this led him to carry out pioneering studies into how behaviour influences emotion Similarly, social psychologist Solomon Asch's work into the influence of group pressure on perception may have been driven by a childhood experience. When he was eight years old, Asch participated in a religious ceremony in which his grandmother poured a glass of wine and then suggested that the prophet Elijah would take a sip. As a result of this comment, Asch thought that he saw the level of the wine becoming lower. To maximize the chances of such break-throughs, psychologists should venture beyond the laboratory, search out surprising and counter-intuitive phenomena, ask unusual questions, study neglected topics, and cultivate a sense of curiosity and openness about themselves and others.

In Chapter 2, we then examined how psycholo-gists have developed a unique methodological toolkit, and how understanding these techniques boosts critical thinking. Two strands of this work have frequently appeared throughout the book and it seems likely that both will play an important role in the future. First, to improve study quality, psychologists are being encouraged both to out-line their methods before they conduct a piece of research (a procedure known as pre-registration) and to replicate each other's work. Second, psy-chology is becoming increasingly aware of the need to involve a more diverse range of researchers and participants, and to pay greater attention to the importance of culture. Both strands of work are vital and will help to ensure that psychology is meaningful to far more people in the future.

Chapter 3 explored how researchers debunk psychology-based myths and examine why people develop such beliefs (including the role played by social media, self-identity, and the need to belong).

Conclusion

The recent, and dramatic, rise of belief in conspiracy theories and fake news makes this work more relevant and important than ever before. Future research in this area could involve identifying popular mind myths in a wide range of real-world contexts, including jury decision making, job interviews, dating, personality testing, education, parenting, mental health, and medicine. In addition, this work could examine the degree to which these ideas influence people's lives, and how to encourage people to adopt a more evidence-based approach to sorting fact from fiction.

Chapter 4 examined how psychology helps to inform and resolve important debates. This work is especially relevant to many present-day concerns. Political opinions have become more extreme and divisive; climate change has emphasized the need for sustainable lifestyles; social justice movements have highlighted systemic inequalities; and the COVID-19 pandemic has induced a sense of uncertainty and change. Psychology has the potential to make major contributions to all these areas and many more. Some aspects of this work are likely to prove challenging. For much of my career, I carried out controversial work into the possible existence of paranormal phenomena. This research often involved questioning people's cherished beliefs and

Conclusion

> ## REPORTING RELEVANCE
>
> Academic papers traditionally contain sections in which researchers explain the background to their work, outline their methods and results, and discuss their findings. Although it's possible to explore the relevance of research within this structure, it is not required. To help tackle the issue, some journals have added an extra section (sometimes called the 'Public Interest Statement') that explicitly asks authors to reflect on why their work matters. This section could be incorporated into all psychology articles and authors could be encouraged to reflect on several key issues, such as why they investigated a certain topic, whether the work is intrinsically interesting or counter-intuitive, and whether it makes the world a better place.

experiences, and resulted in several long-running disputes. As such, I can understand why some researchers might wish to avoid such confrontation. However, it is vital that psychologists with the relevant expertise are encouraged to contribute to important debates and controversies.

The final chapter focused on how psychology enriches lives and improves society. This work is especially important given the increased need for change in many areas, including providing support to those with mental health issues, promoting physical health, reducing unemployment, fostering equality and justice, ensuring sustainability, and building strong communities. Clearly, future work in this area will benefit from researchers exploring real-world issues and developing effective solutions. This approach is often especially effective when psychologists are informed by their lived experiences. For instance, during the 1940s, African American psychologists Mamie and Kenneth Clark investigated self-worth among African American children, and their work helped to make segregation in public schools unconstitutional.[2] Much more recently, Greta Defeyter has described how her first-hand experience of poverty resulted in her studying food insecurity, including investigating the effects of holiday hunger on educational learning loss, and how school breakfast clubs can boost children's academic performance.[3]

One final thought. Psychology is very flexible and so has the potential to allow researchers to study topics that they find personally interesting. As I explained at the start of this book, I have long been fascinated with magic, and in my professional life I have explored the science of conjuring and illusion. Similarly, my colleague Peter Lovatt used to work as a professional dancer and now studies the psychology of dance. Likewise, the well-known psychologist Elizabeth Loftus became interested in eyewitness testimony, in part, because she is a fan of crime novels and courtroom dramas. With a little bit of imagination, the same approach can be used to explore almost any area. For instance, someone with a love of music might examine whether listening to improvisational jazz makes people more creative, or a person into interior design might investigate why certain colour combinations are especially pleasing, or those fascinated by fashion might explore how clothing impacts on self-identity. In my experience, psychologists adopting this approach often bring a sense of passion and insight to their work and are more likely to produce meaningful research.

Our journey is coming to an end and I hope that you have enjoyed discovering why I believe that psychology matters. During our time together, we have explored how psychologists uncover important insights into the mind, challenge popular myths, help to resolve important debates, change people's lives, and improve society. We have also encountered many examples of the exciting and meaningful work carried out in these areas, including how it helps those with mental health issues, promotes happiness, maximizes children's academic potential, encourages sustainability, and reduces prejudice. Psychology is still a relatively young discipline, and these findings are only the tip of the iceberg. There is still so much more to discover, and I believe that the future is bright. As we part company, my hope is that you will continue to celebrate psychology that matters, and uncover even more remarkable insights into the most astonishing, complex, annoying, strange, exciting, innovative, frustrating, and wonderful object in the entire universe: you.

Notes

Chapter 1 How Does Your Mind
Really Work?

1 A.D. Cornell, 'An experiment in apparitional observation and findings', *Journal of the Society for Psychical Research*, 40(701) (1959), 120–124; A.D. Cornell, 'Further experiments in apparitional observation', *Journal of the Society for Psychical Research*, 40(706) (1959), 409–418.

2 U. Neisser, 'The control of information pickup in selective looking', in A.D. Pick (Ed.), *Perception and its development: A tribute to Eleanor J. Gibson* (pp. 201–219). Hillsdale, NJ: Lawrence Erlbaum Associates, 1979.

3 D.J. Simons & C.F. Chabris, 'Gorillas in our midst: Sustained inattentional blindness for dynamic events', *Perception*, 28 (1999), 1059–1074.

4 I. Hyman, S. Boss, B. Wise, K. McKenzie, & J. Caggiano, 'Did you see the unicycling clown? Inattentional blindness while walking and talking on

a cell phone', *Applied Cognitive Psychology*, 24(5) (2009), 597–607.

5 A. Tversky & D. Kahneman, 'Judgment under uncertainty: Heuristics and biases', *Science*, *185* (1974), 1124–1131.

6 For more information, see J. Shepperd, W. Malone, & K. Sweeny, 'Exploring causes of the self-serving bias', *Social and Personality Psychology Compass*, 2 (2008), 895–908.

7 This game is based on work described in: P. Watson, 'On the failure to eliminate hypotheses in a conceptual task', *Quarterly Journal of Experimental Psychology*, *12*(3) (1960), 129–140.

8 Based on: M. Snyder & W.B. Swann, 'Hypothesis-testing processes in social interaction', *Journal of Personality and Social Psychology*, *36* (1978), 1202–1212.

9 M. Workman, 'An empirical study of social media exchanges about a controversial topic: Confirmation bias and participant characteristics', *Journal of Social Media in Society*, 7(1) (2018), 381–400.

10 B. Fischhoff & R. Beyth, '"I knew it would happen": Remembered probabilities of once–future things', *Organizational Behavior and Human Performance*, *13* (1975), 1–16.

11 A.-L. Sellier, I. Scopelliti, & C.K. Morewedge, 'Debiasing training improves decision making in the field', *Psychological Science*, *30*(9) (2019), 1371–1379.

12 B. Latane & J. Darley, 'Bystander "apathy"', *American Scientist*, 57 (1969), 244–268.

13 R. Philpot, L.S. Liebst, M. Levine, W. Bernasco, & M.R. Lindegaard, 'Would I be helped? Cross-national CCTV footage shows that intervention is the norm in public conflicts', *American Psychologist*, 75(1) (2020), 66–75; P. Fischer, J.I. Krueger, T. Greitemeyer, *et al.*, 'The bystander-effect: A meta-analytic review on bystander intervention in dangerous and non-dangerous emergencies', *Psychological Bulletin*, 137(4) (2011), 517–537.

14 A.N.M. Leung, 'To help or not to help: Intervening in cyberbullying among Chinese cyber-bystanders', *Frontiers in Psychology*, 12 (2021), 483250.

Chapter 2 A Unique Toolkit

1 K. Demirci, M. Akgönül, & A. Akpinar, 'Relationship of smartphone use severity with sleep quality, depression, and anxiety in university students', *Journal of Behavioral Addictions*, 4(2) (2015), 85–92; Z. Zhang & W.A. Chen, 'Systematic review of the relationship between physical activity and happiness', *Journal of Happiness Studies*, 20 (2019), 1305–1322; T.L. Scott, B.M. Masser, & N.A. Pachana, 'Positive aging benefits of home and community gardening activities: Older adults report enhanced self-esteem, productive endeavours, social engagement and exercise', *SAGE Open Medicine*, 8 (2020), 2050312120901732.

2 R.V. Levine & A. Norenzayan, 'The pace of life in 31 countries', *Journal of Cross-Cultural Psychology*, 30(2) (1999), 178–205.

3 M.G. Frank & T. Gilovich, 'The dark side of self- and

social perception: Black uniforms and aggression in professional sports', *Journal of Personality and Social Psychology*, 54(1) (1988), 74–85.

4 L. Mattar, N. Farran, J. Abi Kharma, & N. Zeeni, 'Movie violence acutely affects food choices in young adults', *Eating Behaviors*, 33 (2019), 7–12.

Chapter 3 Myth Busting

1 See, for example: National Research Council, *The polygraph and lie detection*, Washington, DC: The National Academies Press, 2003.

2 R. Wiseman, C. Watt, L. ten Brinke, S. Porter, S.-L. Couper, & C. Rankin. 'The eyes don't have it: Lie detection and neuro-linguistic programming', *PLoS ONE*, 7(7) (2012), e40259.

3 This work is reviewed in: A. Vrij, M. Hartwig, & P.A. Granhag, 'Reading lies: Nonverbal communication and deception', *Annual Review of Psychology*, 70(1) (2019), 295–317.

4 The Global Deception Research Team, 'A world of lies', *Journal of Cross-Cultural Psychology*, 37(1) (2006), 60–74.

5 S.K. Lower, 'Treating astrology's claims with all due gravity', *Nature*, 447 (2007), 538.

6 For a review, see G. Dean & I.W. Kelly, 'Is astrology relevant to consciousness and psi?', *Journal of Consciousness Studies*, 10(6–7) (2003), 175–198.

7 B.R. Forer, 'The fallacy of personal validation: A classroom demonstration of gullibility', *Journal of Abnormal Psychology*, 44 (1949), 118–121.

8 A.H. Hastorf & H. Cantril, 'They saw a game: A case study', *Journal of Abnormal and Social Psychology*, *49* (1954), 129–134.

9 K.A. Wade, M. Garry, J.D. Read, & D.S. Lindsay, 'A picture is worth a thousand lies: Using false photographs to create false childhood memories', *Psychonomic Bulletin and Review*, *9* (2002), 597–603.

10 E.F. Loftus & J.E. Pickrell, 'The formation of false memories', *Psychiatric Annals*, *25* (1995), 720–725; see also I.E. Hyman, T.H. Husband, & F.J. Billings, 'False memories of childhood experiences', *Applied Cognitive Psychology*, *9* (1995), 181–195.

11 L.B. Pham & S.E. Taylor, 'From thought to action: Effects of process-versus outcome-based mental simulations on performance', *Personality and Social Psychology Bulletin*, *25* (1999), 250–260.

12 G. Oettingen & D. Mayer, 'The motivating function of thinking about the future: Expectations versus fantasies', *Journal of Personality and Social Psychology*, *83* (2002), 1198–1212.

13 Visualization is a common and effective technique in sports coaching: see, for example, R.N. Singer, D. Symons Downs, L. Bouchard, & D. de la Pena, 'The influence of a process versus outcome orientation on tennis performance and knowledge', *Journal of Sport Behavior*, *24* (2001), 213–222; and K.M. Kingston & L. Hardy, 'Effects of different types of goals on processes that support performance', *Sport Psychology*, *11* (1997), 277–293.

Chapter 4 Informing and Resolving Debate

1 D. Bem, 'Feeling the future: Experimental evidence for anomalous retroactive influences on cognition and affect', *Journal of Personality and Social Psychology*, 100(3) (2011), 407–425.

2 S.J. Ritchie, R. Wiseman, & C.C. French, 'Failing the future: Three unsuccessful attempts to replicate Bem's "retroactive facilitation of recall" effect', *PLoS ONE*, 7(3)(2012), e33423.

3 D. Bem, P. Tressoldi, T. Rabeyron, & M. Duggan, 'Feeling the future: A meta-analysis of 90 experiments on the anomalous anticipation of random future events', *F1000Research*, 4 (2015), 1188.

4 See, for example: E.J. Wagenmakers, D. Wetzels, R. Borsboom, & H.L. van der Maas, 'Why psychologists must change the way they analyze their data: The case of psi. Comment on Bem (2011)', *Journal of Personality and Social Psychology*, 100(3) (2011), 426–432.

5 M. Schlitz, D. Bem, D. Marcusson-Clavertz, *et al.*, 'Two replication studies of a time-reversed (psi) priming task and the role of expectancy in reaction times', *Journal of Scientific Exploration*, 35(1) (2021), 65–90.

6 See, for example, J. Alcock, 'Give the null hypothesis a chance: Reasons to remain doubtful about the existence of psi', *Journal of Consciousness Studies*, 10(6–7) (2003), 29–50; E. Cardeña, 'The experimental evidence for parapsychological phenomena: A review', *The American Psychologist*, 73(5) (2018), 663–677.

7 M.P. Walker, C. Liston, J.A. Hobson, & R. Stickgold, 'Cognitive flexibility across the sleep–wake cycle: REM-sleep enhancement of anagram problem solving', *Brain Research. Cognitive Brain Research*, 14(3) (2002), 317–324.

8 D. Barrett, 'The "committee of sleep": A study of dream incubation for problem solving', *Dreaming*, 3(2) (1993), 115–122.

9 C.E. Hill, J. Zack, T. Wonnell, *et al.*, 'Structured brief therapy with a focus on dreams or loss for clients with troubling dreams and recent losses', *Journal of Counseling Psychology*, 47 (2000), 90–101; M.R. Kolchakian & C.E. Hill, 'Dream interpretation with heterosexual dating couples', *Dreaming*, 12(1) (2002), 1–16.

10 M.R. Olsen, M. Schredl, & I. Carlsson, 'Conscious use of dreams in waking life (nontherapy setting) for decision-making, problem-solving, attitude formation, and behavioral change', *Dreaming*, 30(3), 257–266.

11 G. Perry, *Behind the shock machine: The untold story of the notorious Milgram psychology experiments*, New York: The New Press, 2013.

12 T. Blass, 'The Milgram paradigm after 35 years: Some things we now know about obedience to authority', *Journal of Applied Social Psychology*, 29(5) (1999), 955–978.

13 J.L. Beauvois, D. Courbet, & D. Oberlé, 'The prescriptive power of the television host: A transposition of Milgram's obedience paradigm to the context of TV game show', *European Review of Applied Psychology*, 62(3) (2012), 111–119.

14 S.D. Reicher, S. A. Haslam, & J.R. Smith, 'Working towards the experimenter: Reconceptualizing obedience within the Milgram paradigm as identification-based followership', *Perspectives on Psychological Science*, 7 (2012), 315–324.

15 S. Gibson, 'Milgram's obedience experiments: A rhetorical analysis', *British Journal of Social Psychology*, 52 (2013), 290–309.

16 T. Blass, *The man who shocked the world: The life and legacy of Stanley Milgram*, New York: Basic Books, 2004.

17 For a summary of this work, see M.S. Gazzaniga, *The bisected brain*, New York: Appleton-Century-Crofts, 1970.

18 For an overview of this work, see V. Rosen, 'One brain. Two minds? Many questions', *Journal of Undergraduate Neuroscience Education: JUNE: A Publication of FUN, Faculty for Undergraduate Neuroscience*, 16(2) (2018), R48–R50; and E.H.F. de Haan, P.M. Corballis, S.A. Hillyard, *et al.*, 'Split-brain: What we know now and why this is important for understanding consciousness', *Neuropsychological Review*, 30 (2020), 224–233.

19 C.S. Dweck, *Mindset: How you can fulfil your potential* (Rev. ed.), London: Robinson, 2017.

20 L. Blackwell, K. Trzesniewski, & C.S. Dweck, 'Implicit theories of intelligence predict achievement across an adolescent transition: A longitudinal study and an intervention', *Child Development*, 78 (2007), 246–263.

21 C.M. Mueller & C.S. Dweck, 'Intelligence praise can undermine motivation and performance', *Journal of Personality and Social Psychology, 75* (1998), 33–52.

22 Y. Li & T.C. Bates, 'You can't change your basic ability, but you work at things, and that's how we get hard things done: Testing the role of growth mindset on response to setbacks, educational attainment, and cognitive ability', *Journal of Experimental Psychology: General, 148*(9) (2019), 1640–1655.

23 C.S. Dweck & D.S. Yeager, 'A simple re-analysis overturns a "failure to replicate" and highlights an opportunity to improve scientific practice: Commentary on Li and Bates (2019)', unpublished paper, doi:10.13039/100000071.

24 V.F. Sisk, A.P. Burgoyne, J. Sun, J.L. Butler, & B.N. Macnamara, 'To what extent and under which circumstances are growth mind-sets important to academic achievement? Two meta-analyses', *Psychological Science, 29*(4) (2018), 549–571.

25 D.S. Yeager & C.S. Dweck, 'What can be learned from growth mindset controversies?', *The American Psychologist, 75*(9) (2020), 1269–1284.

26 OECD, *PISA 2018 results (Volume III): What school life means for students' lives*, PISA, OECD Publishing, 2019. https://doi.org/10.1787/ acd78851-en.

27 D.S. Yeager, P. Hanselman, G.M. Walton, *et al.*, 'A national experiment reveals where a growth mindset improves achievement', *Nature, 573* (2019), 364–369.

28 D.S. Yeager, J.M. Carroll, J. Buontempo, *et al.*,

'Teacher mindsets help explain where a growth mindset intervention does and doesn't work', *Psychological Science*, 33(1) (2022), 18–32.

Chapter 5 Creating a Better World

1 The upstream/downstream analogy is credited to medical sociologist Irving Zola in J.B. McKinlay, 'A case for refocusing upstream: The political economy of illness', *Applying Behavioral Science to Cardiovascular Risk: Conference Proceedings of the American Heart Association* (1975), 7–17.

2 G.W. Fairweather, D.H. Sanders, H. Maynard, & D.L. Cressler, *Community life for the mentally ill: An alternative to institutional care*, New York: Aldine, 1969.

3 S. Zlotowitz, C. Barker, O. Moloney, & C. Howard, 'Service users as the key to service change? The development of an innovative intervention for excluded young people', *Child and Adolescent Mental Health*, 21(2) (2016), 102–108.

4 L.A. Jason, O. Glantsman, J. O'Brien, & K. Ramian (Eds.), *Introduction to community psychology: Becoming an agent of change* (2019). Retrieved from: https://press.rebus.community/introductionto communitypsychology/.

5 Y. Paradies, J. Ben, N. Denson, et al., 'Racism as a determinant of health: A systematic review and meta-analysis', *PLoS ONE, 10*(9) (2015), e0138511.

6 J.P. Harrell, S. Hall, & J. Taliaferro, 'Physiological responses to racism and discrimination: An

assessment of the evidence', *American Journal of Public Health*, 93 (2003), 243–248.

7 See, for example, M. Sims, A.V. Diez-Roux, S.Y. Gebrea, *et al.*, 'Perceived discrimination is associated with health behaviours among African-Americans in the Jackson Heart Study', *Journal of Epidemiology and Community Health*, 70(2) (2016), 187–194.

8 B.N. Brownlow, E.E. Sosoo, R.N. Long, L.S. Hoggard, T.I. Burford, & L.K. Hill, 'Sex differences in the impact of racial discrimination on mental health among Black Americans', *Current Psychiatry Reports*, 21(11) (2019), 112.

9 M. Hänze & R. Berger, 'Cooperative learning, motivational effects, and student characteristics: An experimental study comparing cooperative learning and direct instruction in 12th grade physics classes', *Learning and Instruction*, 17 (2007), 29–41; L.R. Tropp & M.A. Prenovost, 'The role of intergroup contact in predicting children's interethnic attitudes: Evidence from meta-analytic and field studies', in S.R. Levy & M. Killen (Eds.), *Intergroup attitudes and relations in childhood through adulthood* (pp. 236–248), London: Oxford University Press, 2008.

10 R.A. Emmons & M.E. McCullough, 'Counting blessings versus burdens: An experimental investigation of gratitude and subjective well-being in daily life', *Journal of Personality and Social Psychology*, 84 (2003), 377–389.

11 For an overview of this work, see C. Peterson & M. Seligman, *Character strengths and virtues: A handbook and classification*, Oxford: Oxford University

Press, 2004. See also F. Gander, R.T. Proyer, W. Ruch, & T. Wyss, 'Strength-based positive interventions: Further evidence for their potential in enhancing well-being', *Journal of Happiness Studies*, *14* (2013), 1241–1259.

12 For a review of this work, see A. Wrzesniewski, N. LoBuglio, J.E. Dutton, & J.M. Berg, 'Job crafting and cultivating positive meaning and identity in work', in A.B. Bakker (Ed.), *Advances in positive organizational psychology* (Advances in Positive Organizational Psychology, Vol. 1, pp. 281–302), Bingley, UK: Emerald Group Publishing Limited, 2013.

13 S. Lyubomirsky, K.M. Sheldon, & D. Schkade, 'Pursuing happiness: The architecture of sustainable change', *Review of General Psychology*, *9* (2005), 111–131.

14 S. Oishi, H.P. Choi, A. Liu, & J.L. Kurtz, 'Experiences associated with psychological richness', *European Journal of Personality, 35* (2020), 754–770.

15 For a general critical view of positive psychology, see B. Ehrenreich, *Bright-sided: How positive thinking is undermining America*, New York: Picador.

16 For an overview of this work, see the book series: Cross-Cultural Advancements in Positive Psychology (Series editor: A. Delle Fave, published by Springer).

17 For a review, see S. van der Linden, E. Maibach, & A. Leiserowitz, 'Improving public engagement with climate change: Five "best practice" insights from psychological science', *Perspectives on Psychological Science, 10*(6) (2015), 758–763.

18 P. Bain, T. Milfont, Y. Kashima, *et al.*, 'Co-benefits of addressing climate change can motivate action around the world', *Nature Climate Change, 6* (2016), 154–157.

19 N.J. Goldstein, R.B. Cialdini, & V. Griskevicius, 'A room with a viewpoint: Using social norms to motivate environmental conservation in hotels', *Journal of Consumer Research, 35*(3) (2008), 472–482.

20 D.A. Small, G. Loewenstein, & P. Slovic, 'Sympathy and callousness: The impact of deliberative thought on donations to identifiable and statistical victims', *Organizational Behavior and Human Decision Processes, 102* (2007), 143–153.

21 C. Skurka, J. Niederdeppe, R. Romero-Canyas, & D. Acup, 'Pathways of influence in emotional appeals: Benefits and tradeoffs of using fear or humor to promote climate change-related intentions and risk perceptions', *Journal of Communication, 68*(1) (2018), 169–193.

Conclusion

1 Although the bystander effect exists, the accuracy of media reports about witnesses hearing the attack have been called into question: R. Manning, M. Levine, & A. Collins, 'The Kitty Genovese murder and the social psychology of helping: The parable of the 38 witnesses', *American Psychologist, 62*(6) (2007), 555–562.

2 R. Kluger, *Simple justice: The history of Brown v.*

Board of Education and Black America's struggle for equality, New York: Random House, 1975.

3 J. Sutton & G. Defeyter, 'I'm one of them', *The Psychologist*, 34 (2021), 38–42.

Further Reading

Introduction

Slater, L. (2005). *Opening Skinner's box: Great psychological experiments of the twentieth century*. London: Bloomsbury.

An unusual and fascinating perspective on some of the best-known experiments in psychology, including Milgram's obedience studies and work into false memory.

Wiseman, R. (2007). *Quirkology*. London: Pan.

I hope that you will forgive me for listing my own book, but if you are interested in my work, this book covers some of my research into lying, magic, and humour.

Further Reading

Flanagan, C., Jarvis, M., & Liddle, R. (2020). *AQA Psychology for A Level Year 1 & AS Student Book*. High Wycombe, UK: Illuminate Publishing.

A great introductory student text, presenting key themes and important research in psychology.

Myers, D., & Dewall, C.N. (2019). *Exploring psychology* (11th ed.). New York: Worth Publishers.

Another wonderful and detailed introduction to every area of psychology.

Banyard, P. (2022). *Controversy and psychology*. London: Routledge.

An important exploration of some of the more negative aspects of psychology, including work related to racism, categorization, warfare, and persuasion.

Sutton, J. (Ed.). *The Psychologist*. The British Psychological Society.

A great monthly magazine providing up-to-date research reports, interviews, discussion, and debate about a wide range of psychological topics.

Further Reading

Chapter 1 How Does Your Mind Really Work?

Simons, D. & Chabris, C. (2010). *The invisible gorilla*. London: Crown.

Produced by the team that created the wonderful basketball viral video, this book outlines how our intuitions can mislead us in many different contexts.

Kahneman, D. (2011). *Thinking, fast and slow*. New York: Farrar, Straus and Giroux.

A wonderful and influential exploration into how we think, and how our biases can sway important decisions and judgements.

Aronson, E. & Aronson, J. (2018). *The social animal* (12th ed.). New York: Worth Publishers.

A classic introduction to social psychology, covering a vast range of topics, including altruism, conformity, obedience, prejudice, attraction, and religion.

Chapter 2 A Unique Toolkit

Rolls, G. (2019). *Classic case studies in psychology*. London: Taylor & Francis.

A great account of the role that case studies play within psychology and how they have yielded valuable insights into thinking, emotions, and behaviour.

Further Reading

Howitt, D. (2019). *Introduction to qualitative research methods in psychology: Putting theory into practice.* London: Pearson.

A comprehensive guide to qualitative research methods, including the underlying philosophy, ethics, methods, and report writing.

Coolican, H. (2018). *Research methods and statistics in psychology.* London: Routledge.

An in-depth look at quantitative research methods. I didn't explore the role of statistics in the chapter, but this book also describes the important role that they play in assessing the outcome of any study.

Keith, K.D. (Ed.). (2018). *Culture across the curriculum: A psychology teacher's handbook.* Cambridge: Cambridge University Press.

An accessible and informative guide to the importance of recognizing the role of culture within all aspects of psychology, including research methods, cognition, development, and personality.

Chambers, C. (2019). *The seven deadly sins of psychology: A manifesto for reforming the culture of scientific practice.* Princeton, NJ: Princeton University Press.

An eye-opening examination of the issues that can hinder psychological research and the importance of tackling these problems, including the role of replication and pre-registration.

Chapter 3 Myth Busting

Lilienfeld, S.O., Lynn, S.J., Ruscio, J., & Beyerstein, B.L. (2010). *50 great myths of popular psychology: Shattering widespread misconceptions about human behavior*. Oxford: Wiley-Blackwell.

A comprehensive overview of enduring mind myths, including work relating to the notion that we only use 10% of our brains, that our memories are highly accurate, and that polygraphs are a reliable way of detecting lies.

Briers, S. (2012). *Psychobabble: Exploding the myths of the self-help generation*. London: Pearson.

A much-needed examination of the myths surrounding the self-help industry, including a critical appraisal of positive thinking, visualization, and some types of psychotherapy.

Della Sala, S. (Ed.). (2007). *Tall tales about the mind and brain: Separating fact from fiction*. Oxford: Oxford University Press.

A great look at lots of psychology-based myths, including work on lying, paranormal belief, graphology, dowsing, and the impact of the full moon.

Chapter 4 *Informing and Resolving Debate*

Watt, C. (2016). *Parapsychology – A beginner's guide.* London: Oneworld Publications.

A balanced and accessible review of experimental work in parapsychology, including research into the alleged existence of extra-sensory perception.

Ralls, E. & Riggs, C. (2019). *The little book of psychology.* Chichester, UK: Summerdale Publishers Ltd.

An informative and fun guide to the many lenses through which psychologists view the human psyche.

Malinowski, J. (2020). *The psychology of dreaming.* London: Routledge.

A lovely overview of research into dreaming, including why we dream, the relationship between dreaming and creativity, and whether it is possible to learn lucid dreaming.

Blass, T. (2004). *The man who shocked the world: The life and legacy of Stanley Milgram.* New York: Basic Books.

Further Reading

A wonderful and highly readable biography of Stanley Milgram, exploring the significant contribution that he made to social psychology.

Perry, G. (2013). *Behind the shock machine: The untold story of the notorious Milgram psychology experiments*. New York: The New Press.

A detailed and fascinating re-evaluation of Milgram's obedience experiments. Taking a deep dive into original sources, Perry questions the validity of this classic research.

Gazzaniga, M.S. (2015). *Tales from both sides of the brain: A life in neuroscience*. New York: Ecco Press.

The engaging autobiography from the 'father of cognitive neuroscience', describing his seminal work with split-brain brain patients and exploring whether the brain's hemispheres are capable of acting independently.

Dweck, C.S. (2017). *Mindset: Changing the way you think to fulfil your potential*. Revised edition. London: Robinson.

A fascinating and ground-breaking exploration of research into growth and fixed mindsets, examining how the concept can be applied within education, business, sport, and relationships.

Further Reading

Chapter 5 Creating a Better World

Pilgrim, D. (2019). *Key concepts in mental health*. London: Sage Publications Ltd.

An accessible overview of theoretical and practical issues surrounding mental health, including the relationship between mental health issues and society.

Wampold, B.E. & Imel, Z.E. (2015). *The great psychotherapy debate: The evidence for what makes psychotherapy work*. London: Routledge.

A classic text exploring the history of psychotherapy, outlining competing models, and discussing the efficacy of these different approaches.

Riemer, M., Reich, S.M., Evans, S.D., Nelson, G. & Prilleltensky, I. (2020). *Community psychology: In pursuit of liberation and wellbeing*. London: Bloomsbury Academic.

Discusses key theories and methods relating to community psychology across a range of cultures and settings, including work into social justice, racism, and homelessness.

Jackson, L.M. (2019). *The psychology of prejudice: From attitudes to social action*. Washington, DC: American Psychological Association.

A comprehensive review of the psychological mechanisms that underpin prejudice, the impact of prejudice on society, and how to create lasting social change.

Owen, A. (2018). *Into the grey zone: Exploring the border between life and death*. London: Guardian Faber Publishing.

A wonderful and moving account of work into the use of brain scanning to communicate with those who are self-aware but locked into their bodies.

Hart, R. (2020). *Positive psychology: The basics*. London: Routledge.

An accessible review of positive psychology, including work into wellbeing, optimism, happiness, the potential to change, character strengths, and positive relationships.

Beattie, G. & McGuire, L. (2018). *The psychology of climate change*. London: Routledge.

An important overview of the changes in attitude and behaviour needed to combat climate change, and the role that psychological research can play in this process.

Further Reading

Conclusion

Sternberg, R. (2020). Intelligence, love, creativity and wisdom. In T. Witkowski (Ed.), *Shaping psychology* (pp. 79–100). Cham, Switzerland: Palgrave Macmillan.

A wonderful interview reflecting on the importance of psychologists moving away from simply pursuing grants and publications, and instead conducting research that is more meaningful and relevant.